P9-DHH-751

HOW TO GET OUT OF DEBT
WITHOUT DESPAIR
AND WITHOUT A LAWYER

HOW TO GET OUT OF DEBT

WITHOUT DESPAIR AND WITHOUT A LAWYER

by Daniel Kaufman

A CORWIN BOOKS PAPERBACK
Pinnacle Books   *Los Angeles*

Bankruptcy forms reproduced by permission
of Julius Blumberg, Inc.

HOW TO GET OUT OF DEBT WITHOUT DESPAIR
AND WITHOUT A LAWYER

Copyright © 1978 by Daniel Kaufman

All rights reserved, including the right to reproduce this book or portions thereof
in any form.

A Corwin Books Paperback edition.
First printing, June 1978

ISBN: 0-89474-014-8
LIBRARY OF CONGRESS CATALOG CARD NO.: 77-92522

Printed in the United States of America

CORWIN BOOKS, a division of
Pinnacle Books, Inc.
One Century Plaza
2029 Century Park East
Los Angeles, California 90067

Contents

PART 3   PERSONAL BANKRUPTCY

PART 4   BANKRUPTABILIA

PART 5   APPENDICES

INTRODUCTION

CHAPTER ONE

About This Book

Being in debt is by no means an incurable disease. There are a number of honest, straightforward remedies that don't require you to borrow more money or to hire a lawyer. This book will show them to you. But it won't do everything.

It won't tell you why you're in debt and crusade for laws to protect consumers who have champagne tastes on a beer budget. Nobody knows better than you the reasons you're in debt. Analysis is not the object—*getting out* of debt is, and this book can help you tremendously.

It won't give you lots of advice about managing your money. Everybody knows Cadillacs cost more than Fords, that day-old bread isn't too stale, and that movies cost less if you watch them on TV. Unlike many other publications, moreover, this book doesn't ignore the fact that you didn't answer that telephone out of fear that it was somebody to whom you owe money (a creditor). Only a debtor—you—knows what hell it is to be constantly avoiding bill collectors, and this book can get them off your back.

But this book is not for everybody. It's not for people whose debts are all (or almost all) business related. If you're one of the nine out of every ten small businessmen who didn't make it, don't be too surprised. If there is comfort in your brand of financial distress, it must be in the knowledge that you're normal.

This book is not for cheaters. Debt relief, including bankruptcy, is a very serious business. One slip, and you might be wishing that the knock at the door was the garden variety bill collector—not the FBI.

This book *is* a serious, practical, and proven plan for debtor relief. It does not promise instant miracles, but it does promise that the study and application of the techniques detailed in it will immediately help solve your financial problems. It is for diligent, honest people who, for their own legitimate reasons, owe more money than they can pay, and who sincerely want to do something positive about it, without building up more debts in the process.

HOW TO USE THIS BOOK

Read the entire book cover to cover, at one uninterrupted sitting. It won't take too long, and it may be one of the most productive evenings you ever spend. Put it down, and do the same thing a few nights later.

There are good reasons for doing this. For one thing, there is some complicated material here that will take a while to digest. You may not follow everything the first time through, and you're not expected to. Nothing substantial comes easily, and that includes relief from serious financial troubles.

Secondly, much of what's in the earlier chapters won't begin to make sense until you read the later ones. It is vital that you understand all the reasons behind the techniques revealed in this book, and only a close reading of the later chapters will give you this understanding.

And be sure that when you're reading the later chapters, you don't forget what you read in the earlier ones. Don't be misled by the table of contents: Parts II and III may appear to be unrelated, and you might be surprised, while reading Part II, that bankruptcy is so infrequently mentioned. The truth of the matter is, however, that relief techniques *short* of bankruptcy are directly tied to relief *in* bankruptcy. *The steps you take to avoid bankruptcy are the steps you must take in expectation of bankruptcy.*

That statement may sound like a contradiction in terms, but don't try to figure it out now. Just memorize it, and chew it over for a few days. The meaning will come, and you won't want to change a word!

Adapt the book's forms and techniques to fit your own case. Plagiarize this book as much as you want, but realize that not only is John Doe nobody, but nobody is John Doe. The sample letters and forms in this book are merely guidelines, to be modified as your circumstances require.

CHAPTER TWO

A Brief History
of Consumer Credit

If you have blamed your stars for making you a debtor, don't be too harsh on them. Thank them instead for putting your debtor-hood in twentieth-century America, for if there was ever a time and place to be in debt, this is probably it.

Included among the bleakest chapters in American history must be the treatment of persons in debt. Unlike today, until shortly before the Civil War, inability to pay debts was a criminal offense, and a debtor was no better off than a common thief.

If you've visited colonial Williamsburg, you've seen the stocks in which debtors were confined. Those facilities, however, must have seemed humane compared to the more notorious prisons for debtors, such as Newgate Prison near Granby, Connecticut, and similar prisons in Northampton and Worcester, Massachusetts, and in Philadelphia.

Americans were hardly the first to treat debtors so harshly, however. According to certain passages in both the Old Testament and the New Testament, debtors in Biblical times were *enslaved* for nonpayment.[1]

[1] 2 Kings 4:1 "Thy servant my husband is dead . . . and the creditor is come to take unto him my two sons to be bondmen."

Matthew 18:24, 25 "And when he had begun to reckon, one was brought unto him, which owed him ten thousand talents. But forasmuch as he had not to pay, his lord commanded him to be sold, and his wife, and children, and all that he had, and payment to be made."

6

The first state to abolish debtors' prisons was Kentucky—in 1821. The last was Massachusetts, that bastion of liberalism, in 1857. But the abolition of debtors' prisons was merely one element of "progress" in the history of debtors' rights. Although much archaic language has been retained in the law, practices have indeed been reformed. And, with the recent trend toward consumerism, debtors today, while not yet on a par with creditors, are enjoying fairer treatment than ever before.

This is not to say, however, that today's market is the debtor's. Despite all the progress, creditors still don't lean over backwards to tell debtors what their rights are. They can still put a lot of legal pressure on you, and the agony you suffer from the loss of property or your job may make Newgate prison seem inviting. Moreover, because the creditor/debtor relationship today is increasingly anonymous, bill collectors for Megalopolis Enterprises, Inc. can, and will, use tactics that Mom and Pop's grocery wouldn't stand for.

Relief *is* available. It will require some hard decisions, some tough work, and some potentially embarrassing revelations. But you will triumph and (like Hamlet) will emerge nobler and (unlike Hamlet) much, much wealthier.

2

GETTING OUT OF DEBT WITHOUT DECLARING BANKRUPTCY

In this section we will examine how you can obtain total financial relief short *of declaring bankruptcy. The steps outlined here are not only possible alternatives to bankruptcy but are also the preliminary steps to declaring bankruptcy. The bankruptcy methods outlined in Part III are based on the assumption that you have taken these steps and, unless you have done so, your bankruptcy—if it comes to that—will not be as successful as it could be.*

Basically, the steps outlined in this section will get the creditors off your back—at least for an essential four months. They'll get their money, but less of your blood, sweat, and tears.

CHAPTER THREE

Step One: Inventory Your Estate[1]

You don't need a special form to do this. Just get out a large sheet of paper, and at the top write *Assets*. Under that heading, list everything you own that has any value at all. Try to be systematic in order not to overlook anything. If you can't decide whether something has value, ask yourself not how much *you* would pay for it, but how much a *stranger* would. Opposite each asset write its fair market value (FMV). FMV is the amount that a willing purchaser, with knowledge of all the facts, would give a willing seller in an open marketplace.[2] "Sentimental value" is a contradiction in terms. Sentiment *has* no value (at least in this context). If you're unsure about the value of something, assign it the lowest conceivable value (and you're probably still too high). One doesn't have to go to many auctions and flea markets to see the sad fate of other people's treasures. Just imagine Grandfather's portrait up on the auction block, and try to contain

[1]You don't have to be dead to have an estate. What the word means is everything you own, assets *and* liabilities, in the aggregate.

[2]Don't reduce the figure by the amount you may owe on it. For example, if you paid $4000 for your car, and like models are now selling on used-car lots for $1500, write down $1500, despite the fact that you still owe $500 on it. (Incidentally, if that were the case, you would be said to have $1000 "equity" in the car: FMV, less amount owed.)

your resentment toward the giggling teenagers who bought it for a dollar.

When you've listed everything you can think of, turn to Appendix A in the back of this book, and use the items listed there as a checklist for anything you might have overlooked. Be sure to look over the list of frequently forgotten assets. There just might be something there that will send you running to the attic. When the list is complete, *total* the values of the assets listed. Call that figure *Total Assets.*

On the next page, list *Liabilities.* These are debts you owe.[3] First jot down as many as you can think of, then look over the list in Appendix B. For the amount to enter, write down the amount you'd have to come up with to pay off the entire sum. You should be able to figure most of these closely. The only mystery might be the home mortgage. To find out how much you owe, call the mortgage department of the bank that has your mortgage, and ask for a pay-off figure as of a date about two weeks away.[4] If the figure they give you is hardly less than the total amount of the original mortgage, don't be too surprised.

If there are debts you are not certain you owe, list them. You may have successfully repressed their memory, thanks to sympathetic creditors. Add these figures up, call the sum *Total Liabilities,* and pour yourself a drink.

The third page will be devoted to income and, as you have no doubt guessed, the fourth will be expenses. It will make things a lot easier if you list both on either an all-monthly or an all-weekly basis. Pick one or the other, and if you can't decide, use monthly figures.

There are 4.33 weeks in a month (52 ÷ 12). Thus, if you earn $285.00 a week, multiply that figure by 4.33, and list your monthly income as $1234.05. If your unemployment check is $160.00 every two weeks, divide by 2, then multiply by 4.33, which equals $346.40 per month. Be sure to include any income you might receive annually

---

[3]Don't confuse liabilities with recurring expenses. If the rent isn't due yet, you don't yet owe it, and it isn't a liability. But if you didn't pay last month's rent, you do owe it and it is a liability.

[4]These inquiries usually indicate that the house is about to be sold. If you're well known at the bank, some rumors might start circulating that could motivate the bank to stop hassling you about late payments, since they'll think they're getting their money in two weeks.

(don't count on gifts), and translate that amount into monthly figures. Add them all up, and you have *Total Monthly Income.*

Next do page 4—*Expenses.* If you figured income on a monthly basis, do the same with expenses. If food costs you $50 per week, multiply $50 times 4.33, and list your monthly food bill as $216.50. And be sure not to overlook *annual* bills, like your homeowner's insurance premium or club dues. Divide those by twelve. Add all your expenses up to determine your *Total Monthly Expenses.*

Before you go on, take one more look at the items listed in Appendices A and B. Be sure you haven't overlooked any asset, liability, source of income, or regular expense.

CHAPTER FOUR

Step Two: Make Yourself Judgment Proof

Imagine the following situation. Your five-year-old child has discovered, much to his delight and your distress, a deck of cards, and is offering to teach you a new game he has invented. With enthusiasm and gratitude, you take a farewell glimpse at the instant replay, and succumb.

Twelve cards are dealt into each hand; the remaining cards are placed face down between you. The rules, you are told, are simple: the object of the game is to get rid of red cards ("bad" ones) and retain black cards ("good" ones), through a process of alternately drawing and discarding. When a joker is drawn by either player, "Joker!" is shouted, whereupon each person lays down his hand. The player with the fewest red cards wins.

It doesn't take a Charles Goren to devise a winning strategy: retain spades or clubs as you draw them and discard hearts or diamonds. With a few rounds of practice, you begin to feel more secure, and with each "bad" card that is swapped for a "good" one, you become decreasingly worried by the imminent squeals of "Joker!"

Your hand is becoming judgment proof. You and your child both know that as long as your hand (assets) consists entirely of black

16

cards (exempt assets), when you get sued ("Joker!"), you can't possibly lose.

The Congress of the United States and the legislatures of every state have decided that certain assets, like black cards, are practically sacred and *cannot* be reached by anybody who sues you and gets a judgment against you.[1] Politicians are generally humane (if not human) and realize that putting families out on the street helps neither their vote appeal nor the public treasury, which would then have to feed and house those families made destitute. These laws obviously are designed for the protection of families suddenly faced with a financial catastrophe. Once the catastrophe strikes ("Joker!"), however, it's too late for them to convert their assets into exempt ones.

What assets are exempt? The answer is slightly more involved than "black cards," but not incomprehensibly so. There are two categories of exempt assets: (1) those declared exempt by federal law, and (2) those declared exempt by the law of your state.

EXEMPT ASSETS UNDER FEDERAL LAW

Under federal law, the following assets are exempt from levy or seizure by creditors ("U.S.C." stands for United States Code, the body of federal laws, and the numbers refer to chapters and sections):

(1) 10 U.S.C. 1035: Savings of a member of the Armed Forces on permanent duty outside the United States, deposited with his or her branch of the service.

(2) 38 U.S.C. 3101: Payments of benefits due or to become due under any law administered by the Veterans Administration.

(3) 38 U.S.C. 175: Lands acquired under the provisions of federal homestead laws.

(4) 22 U.S.C. 1104: Foreign Service retirement and disability funds.

[1]A judgment is a determination by a court having proper authority that you owe someone money, and how much.

17

(5) 45 U.S.C. 228(1): Railroad retirement benefits and pensions.

(6) 50 U.S.C. 403(263): Central Intelligence Agency Retirement and Disability Fund moneys.

(7) 5 U.S.C. 8346: Moneys payable under the Civil Service Retirement and Disability Fund.

(8) 33 U.S.C. 916: Benefits payable under the Longshoremen's and Harbor Workers' Compensation Act.

(9) 42 U.S.C. 407: Monies paid or payable under Social Security Old-Age, Survivors, and Disability Insurance Trust Fund.

(10) 33 U.S.C. 775: Payments to widows of employees of the U.S. Lighthouse Service.

EXEMPT ASSETS UNDER STATE LAW

Exemptions under state law are not uniform and vary from state to state. There are, however, many similarities. In most states, the following assets are exempt from seizure by creditors: tools and implements of your trade, household furnishings, wearing apparel, and homesteads.[2]

Appendix C lists by state those assets that have been declared by the state legislatures to be beyond the reach of creditors who have obtained judgments against you (they are called judgment creditors). The entire list makes interesting, if not amusing, reading, and the era

[2]Obviously, assets owned by somebody else—like your spouse—can't be seized to satisfy claims against you, unless you transferred the ownership of those assets for the purpose of defrauding your creditors. Subject to that exception, there's absolutely nothing illegal about having the house or the car in your spouse's name. Beware, however, of a frequently made mistake: don't transfer anything into his or her name if there is the slightest chance of a divorce in your future. Your best bet for the real estate you live in is homestead (more about that later). The rest of the real estate can go into the spouse's name only if it isn't obvious that you're making the transfer to avoid the creditors, and the two of you are very, very happily married.

in which many of these laws first appeared on the books is readily apparent. Moreover, many of the decisions of courts that have been called on to interpret these laws are equally as colorful, and often perplexing.

For instance, debate over the question of whether jewelry qualifies as "wearing apparel" has produced some curious decisions. A federal court in Illinois once decreed that a diamond shirt stud, watch, and ring were included in "wearing apparel" when they were purchased for "actual wear" and not as "mere ornaments." A Texas court, on the other hand, stated that a diamond stud was wearing apparel "where it was worn habitually by the bankrupt to keep his shirt together."

If this form of reasoning were to prevail through the law of debtor and creditor rights, no doubt a gaping loophole would be obvious. Under that reasoning, what matters is the function to which a potentially exempt asset is put, rather than its form. Thus, if you deliver newspapers for a living, using that logic you should trade the Ford in for a Lincoln, and keep tossing 'em from your power windows. But these are old, rather discredited cases, and you are not likely to prevail if you rely on them.

The point is that there is much flexibility in this area. If you have time, and you want to know how courts in your state have construed the laws listed in Appendix C, go to your public library and read the annotations following the statute. The librarian can show you how to find them.

A word about homesteads: a homestead is a *form of ownership* of certain property that renders that property beyond the reach of creditors. Not all property that is beyond the reach of creditors is homestead property, but all homestead property is beyond the reach of creditors. To qualify as a homestead, the property must satisfy two requirements: (1) it must be the type of property declared eligible by state law, and (2) it must be owned in the form likewise prescribed by law.

To be eligible for the "homestead" character in practically every state, the property must be—you guessed it—the homestead: that is, the house and adjoining land where the "head of the family" lives. To satisfy the "form" requirement, your deed should contain language specified by the statutes of your state.

19

To create a homestead, *see your lawyer.* Never attempt to affect your ownership of real estate without using one. The slightest flaw in a deed can be fatal, and if you caused the flaw, you would have nowhere to turn. Lawyers make plenty of mistakes, but they carry malpractice insurance to cover them.

To summarize, real estate can be exempt from the claims of creditors. To insure that yours is, see your lawyer. If you don't own any real estate, you don't need to see your lawyer—yet.

One final word: converting your "red cards" into "black" ones *after* you have contracted the debts may not make them exempt as far as those particular debts are concerned. But do it anyway. You haven't thrown out all your credit cards yet, and there's no reason to.

CHAPTER FIVE

Dealing with Your Most Important Debts

STEP THREE: IDENTIFY MOST IMPORTANT CREDITORS

Enter "Paul."

Paul is your ex-wife. He is the tax collector. He is all of your employees to whom you owe back wages. Paul is, in short, your most important creditors. Go back to your inventory labeled *Liabilities* and identify the following kinds of debts:

(1) *Taxes* owed to the federal government, a state, city, county, town, or water district. This includes taxes you know you owe, whether or not you've received a bill for them;

(2) *Wages or commissions* due employees, whether workmen, servants, clerks, etc., whether full-time or part-time;

(3) *Alimony or child support,* whether or not enforcement proceedings have been brought.

The reason that these are your most important creditors will become clear in Part III of this book.

STEP FOUR: PAY MOST IMPORTANT CREDITORS

"How?" you ask. Good question. First, scan your list of assets to see if there's anything there you don't need and can sell. Next, borrow some money. (Remember, it's only "Paul" that has to be paid now. Don't pay anybody else.) Check the following sources for loans, in roughly this order:

(1) Your place of employment. Do you have access to a credit union? Will your employer permit you to borrow against future salary or your pension?

(2) Refinance the house. Sure, interest rates have gone up, but what's most important is how much *per month* housing costs you. You might even check into the possibility of refinancing at a different bank. Say your interest rate is a quaint 5 percent. Some banks are anxious to rewrite those loans for higher interest, and if your bank is one of them, it might be willing to permit you to pay your entire mortgage for about 90 percent of the present outstanding balance. If they're agreeable, go to the bank next door, borrow what you need to pay off the (discounted) mortgage plus enough to pay "Paul." The money you saved on the discount should just about offset the cost of the higher interest rate next door. Work it out with a pencil and paper first, however.

And, if you decide to refinance, you'll need the services of an attorney. While you've got him, have him be sure that your real estate is owned in an exempt form, preferably homestead.

(3) Your life insurance policy. Borrowing against life insurance policies is the best-kept secret this side of The Rock. The insurance companies obviously don't advertise your right to do so because they want the money as badly as you do. Call your agent, and borrow as much as you can. If you die before the loan is repaid, the balance due is simply deducted from the proceeds payable to your named beneficiary.

(4) "Aunt Bertha." If she won't open up her pocketbook, perhaps she will at least be willing to loan you her credit, i.e., to

cosign a promissory note (IOU) for you at the bank. Or, if she's well fixed and likes you, you might convince her that you deserve an advance on your inheritance. Obviously, you have to handle that one very delicately, and a lawyer is a *must*. Use her lawyer, not yours. That way she'll pay the legal fee, and there shouldn't be any dispute if something happens.

(5) Use your credit cards. Interest rates are high, but if you need dollars in a hurry, take a cash advance on a Master Charge, for instance. Credit cards can come in mighty handy.

Several years ago, the loan department of a large commercial bank called in a destitute customer who was hopelessly behind in his car payments. After some polite browbeating, the customer excused himself for a moment and, instead of heading for the men's room, approached a teller, pulled out his Master Charge, and borrowed the maximum. He then returned to the loan department, handed them the cash, and headed toward his car, secure in the knowledge that he had just gained a comforting, if not cheap, reprieve from one financial hassle.

(6) Avoid finance companies.

Assuming that you have now been able to come up with enough to pay "Paul," do it. If you wish, call the source of the loan "Peter," and resist the well-deserved groan.

CHAPTER SIX

Step Five: See a Credit Counselor

Credit counseling is a relatively new concept in the United States. No doubt it owes its birth to the proliferation of easy credit for modern consumers, and it will probably be with us as long as easy credit continues to be available. Basically, a credit counselor is someone who steps into your financial plight, at your invitation, and helps you straighten out your bills without borrowing money. There are two types of credit counselors, and the distinction is vital.

TYPE A

The Type A credit counselor is known by many names. He is often called a "debt pro-rater," "debt liquidator," "consolidator," "debt pooler," etc. As soon as he gets a bad name, he changes it. And that's frequently.

This guy advertises his "services" in publications that financially distressed people are likely to read, and the ad is often characterized by offers to provide an easy solution to your money problems, with payments as low as some ridiculous amount per week with no collateral or endorsers required. If you answer the ad, you learn that

24

after you pay him a substantial fee, he'll promise to get all your creditors to agree to accept a pro rata share on moneys due them. Then you make one "easy" weekly payment to him, and he splits the money with your creditors, in accordance with the agreed-upon plan.

Avoid Type A like the plague. His "service" is a colossal, classic rip-off. People who buy his services as a rule find themselves in worse trouble than before. In fact, at least one very respectable researcher in this area interviewed a number of such customers and found *not one* who was satisfied with the services he received!

How can you spot a Type A credit counselor? For one thing, he advertises incredibly easy solutions to incredibly difficult problems. For another, he charges a substantial fee for his services. Any sum that cannot be called nominal is substantial. (More than $15 per month cannot be called nominal.) Finally, his overall modus operandi is to prey on those noticeably in trouble.

Find—and use—a Type B credit counselor.

TYPE B

There are a number of honest, legitimate credit counseling agencies available. Perhaps the best known, but by no means the only such organization, is the National Foundation for Consumer Credit. At this writing there are more than 1600 NFCC-affiliated credit counseling offices in the United States and Canada. All are bona fide offices.

If you qualify for their services,[1] the credit counselor will go over all your debts with you, verifying each and screening out those that don't require payment. He will then help you draw up a personal or family budget, itemizing each living expense. If relief is possible, the counselor will personally contact your creditors by mail or telephone and obtain each creditor's approval of a pro rata distribution. He will then send out the individual checks when yours arrives each week or month.

Unlike the Type A counselor, the honest credit counselor will charge only a nominal fee, and he won't accept any of your money until the plan is entirely worked out. He will make all the payments

---

[1]Unfortunately, not everybody does. A common reason people are unqualified is that their debts are too high in proportion to their income.

25

on time (assuming you do) and won't fraudulently advertise. Most important, and unlike many Type A counselors, he won't abscond with your money.

Before you nominate the NFCC and its affiliated offices for sainthood, however, it should be pointed out that they are sponsored largely by the people who get you into trouble in the first place: finance companies, banks, and retailers of consumer goods. Obviously, it's not in these folks' best interest for you to be declaring bankruptcy, and they want to help themselves by helping you.

And they do. One recent study showed that the sponsors of NFCC offices received from five to twelve dollars from distressed debtors for every dollar they invested in establishing the counseling agencies. That statistic, however, should not discourage you from using their services. You have practically nothing to lose (not even pride) and everything to gain, and the only reason not to use their services would be if there isn't an office near you. In that event, follow the next step.

CHAPTER SEVEN

Step Six: Make Your Own Debt Arrangement

Being your own credit counselor is the next best thing to having your own credit counselor. The steps to take are not too difficult if you follow these guidelines.

(1) Take out your inventories. Examine *Total Monthly Expenses* and determine which items on that sheet are *musts,* i.e., food, clothing, and shelter. Add up the essential monthly expenses, and subtract that figure from *Total Monthly Income.* The difference is the amount available to pay creditors, on a pro rata basis.

As in the following example, decide how much you can pay each creditor. Don't hesitate to make the figures as low as necessary. Practically every creditor would rather receive a little money regularly than a lot of money irregularly or never.

For example, say you must make the following monthly expenditures that are vital to the health and well-being of your family:

Rent	$210.00
Utilities (incl. heat)	60.00
Telephone	20.00
Food	150.00
Transportation	50.00
Medical care	50.00
Insurance	65.00
Home supplies, clothing, etc.	50.00
TOTAL	$605.00

The following creditors, however, are demanding payments.

Leverett Furniture	$ 300.00
Linda's Linoleum	210.00
Master Charge	700.00
Friendly Finance	2500.00
Dan's Garage	200.00
Last National Bank	750.00
White's Department Store	350.00
Community Hospital	450.00
Discount Draperies	120.00
Uncle Earl	200.00
Alice's Nursery School	220.00
TOTAL	$6000.00

Your take-home pay is $850 per month. After paying your necessary, vital bills, that leaves $245 ($850 minus $605) to divide among eleven creditors demanding a total of $6000.

Now, *pro-rate* each of these debts. That is, determine the amount that you can pay to each, based on the proportion that each represents of the total. For example, if the money you owe Last National Bank represents 12½ percent of the total debt, then allocate 12½ percent of the amount available for payment each month to Last National Bank. Here's a formula. *X* represents the amount you are going to ask each creditor, respectively, to accept:

$$\frac{\text{Amount Available for Payment (A.A.P.)}}{\text{Total Debts (T.D.)}} = \frac{X}{\text{Present Debt (P.D.)}}$$

Or, to say the same thing a different way:

28

$$X = \frac{\text{A.A.P. times P.D.}}{\text{T.D.}}$$

Now apply this formula to one of the debts on the list, and plug in some figures. Let's take Leverett Furniture, the first creditor on the list.

$$X = \frac{\$245 \text{ times } \$300}{\$6000}$$

and, solving for X,

$$X = \frac{\$73,500}{\$6000}$$

$$X = \$12.25\%.$$

Thus, you would ask Mr. Leverett to accept $12.25 per month until your entire debt is paid.

Let's do another one. Friendly Finance is demanding $2500. How much should you offer them per month?

$$X = \frac{\$245 \text{ times } \$2500}{\$6000}$$

$$X = \$102.08.$$

To check your arithmetic, add all your Xs. The total should be your amount available for payment.

	Total Debt	Pro-rated payment (X)
Leverett Furniture	$ 300.00	$ 12.25
Linda's Linoleum	210.00	8.57
Master Charge	700.00	28.58
Friendly Finance	2500.00	102.08
Dan's Garage	200.00	8.17
Last National Bank	750.00	30.63
White's Department Store	350.00	14.29
Community Hospital	450.00	18.38
Discount Draperies	120.00	4.90
Uncle Earl	200.00	8.17
Alice's Nursery School	220.00	8.98
TOTAL	$6000.00	$245.00 (A.A.P.)

29

A little more arithmetic will show you that all these debts will be fully paid in two years.

(2) Write a letter to each creditor. This is the critical part. You've got to elicit lots of sympathy and understanding to get all the creditors to agree on a pro rata plan, and you've got to convince them that going along with your proposal is in *their* best interests. The most common technique is the threat of bankruptcy, and don't hesitate to use it.[1]

Sample letters are contained in Appendix D. As you will note, you can ask for a reduction in payments, a delay of all payments, or both.

It's no secret that marital problems and financial problems often go hand in hand, but be careful not to permit the inference that your marriage is not the happiest and soundest in town. Use "we," and be sure to mention the kids. If any creditor gets wind of a divorce, he won't listen to any tale of woe. Creditors know that D-I-V-O-R-C-E spells nonpayment, and they'll come pounding at your door if they get so much as a hint of imminent divorce.

(3) *Don't* wait for the creditors to write back with a yes or no. Make the first (reduced) payment at once, as a show of good faith (unless, of course, you are asking for a delay on all payments). If they haven't decided whether to approve your proposed arrangement, the arrival of the first check right on schedule will give you the benefit of the doubt.

---

[1]Threatening bankruptcy is an old, old game among businessmen, and sometimes it can backfire. For example, consider a recent case of store X and store Y, competitors in a moderately sized city. The proprietor of X decided he wanted to buy out Y, so he made Y an offer which was agreeable. Then he got on the phone to Y's suppliers, who had extended credit to Y for inventory, and announced that Y was on the verge of bankruptcy, but that he (X) had offered to "help" Y, but could do so only if Y's creditors would agree to accept 50¢ for each dollar Y owed them. They did. The owner of Y then became upset that "such things" were being said about him, and contacted his lawyer, who spotted a loophole in the contract for sale of the business, and it was thereupon cancelled. Mr. Y then mailed 50 percent checks to the suppliers and sold the inventory to regular customers, making a bundle. He was no longer upset.

During the period that your "arrangement" is operative, you may slip behind in a payment or two, or something else might happen to cause the creditor to contact you. In that event, try to convince him how deserving you are of his tears, and *don't* forget the following:

(1) *Don't* sign a paper (frequently called a "confession of judgment") that allows the creditor to get a judgment against you without giving you an opportunity to appear in court.

(2) *Don't* give up any collateral without a court order *and* a signed statement that the creditor won't sue you for a deficiency (the difference between what he can sell the collateral for and the amount you owe him on it). If a truck pulls up and the man demands the refrigerator, require *both* documents.

(3) *Don't* assign your wages.

(4) *Don't* sign any new promissory notes.

Now, let's pause for a minute, and reflect on what's happened up to now. You've written to your creditors (or someone in your behalf has written to them), and they've agreed to accept smaller monthly payments. You were diligent, but during the second month an emergency came up, and you couldn't keep up with the payments. No sweat! You've handled the hard part, and the rest is downhill.

CHAPTER EIGHT

Final Steps

STEP SEVEN: HOLD THE FORT

The object of fort-holding is simply to maintain the status quo. No additional payments are necessary, but effective fort-holding requires a barrage of *communication*. Don't avoid the creditors. Doing so will only make them feel justified in their pursuit. Write, call, visit. Give them more and better explanations, excuses, expectations. Perhaps a post-dated check. (But if you do, write across the top in bold letters, "This is a post-dated check.") Offer *collateral* (something you could live without, like the snowmobile).

Some debts are ignorable, at least temporarily. If you are delinquent in your home mortgage payments, the bank will probably let you stay there three months before starting foreclosure proceedings. Insurance premiums can also be slipped back a month or two, but be sure your policy isn't canceled. Obviously, if you are making payments on something that, on reflection, you neither want nor need, and the seller retained a security interest in it, quit making payments and let him repossess it (but be sure to get a release of a deficiency claim).

Perhaps the best method known, and too infrequently used, is to file complaints about the quality of goods for which a claim is being made against you. For some curious reasons, creditors are reluctant to file suit against you if they think you may have a good defense to the claim. Perhaps the reason is that lawyers who handle collections aren't equipped to prove that a refrigerator *was* working properly, despite your assertions to the contrary. This is not to say that you can escape liability for the debt, but rather that you can gain some valuable time. A suggested letter appears in Appendix D. Modify it to fit your situation.

Examine your goods closely for defects. Certainly you should not try to break something that claims to be unbreakable, or "accidentally" ruin an appliance (after all, you need it yourself). But don't, by any means, stop there. Call your district attorney's office and ask for the name and address of the consumer protection agencies to whom you should write. If you have a legitimate complaint about defective goods or abuse by creditors, write them all. There are also toll-free telephone numbers available in some states.

In your letter to the consumer protection agencies, explain that you believe you have been the victim of some fraudulent/illegal/discriminatory/shocking/questionable/cruel/abusive/despicable/injurious practices by the certain dealer/proprietor/bureau/manufacturer/serviceman, and then explain the reasons for that conclusion. Be sure you can support everything you say with good evidence. You can get into more serious trouble by making statements that aren't true.

Another way to gain time is to report to the Better Business Bureau in your community any unfair or improper harassment that your creditors have been giving you. Put it in writing, and send copies to the creditors.

If you have any nonexempt property left that you don't need, offer it as collateral for any debt if that will satisfy the creditor. As long as you get nasty letters from the creditor or a collection agency, you're at least a month away from a lawsuit. When you get a letter from a lawyer, you should step up your activity.

Don't ignore a lawyer's letter! Write back just before the deadline for payment expires and complain of something defective with the goods or services for which he is trying to collect the bill. He won't know anything about your claims, and he'll have to call or see his client, the creditor, to get the other side of the story. If you've ever known a lawyer, you know that step alone will use up a good week or two. Ideally, you should get a lawyer to assert your claim that the merchandise or service was defective. Man knoweth no delay like that born of lawyers.

If you think you can't afford a lawyer to defend a collection claim, consider these possibilities: (1) a legal-services attorney. They're swamped with cases just like yours, but maybe you can convince him or his paralegal assistant to write to the creditor's lawyer. Or, if you can't find a legal-services office, then (2) call up a local lawyer and ask the secretary for the names of the newest, youngest attorneys in town. If she asks why, tell the truth: you've got a good defense to a creditor's claim, but can't affort to pay a substantial legal fee. Young lawyers are frequently starving and will work hard for a minimal fee. In any event, he or she will probably write a "lawyer's letter" back to the creditor's lawyer, thus gaining some valuable time for you.

Meanwhile, back to the fort-holding. There are several essential "don'ts" that you must observe if you are to remain beyond the long arm of your clamoring creditors:

(1) If a bank is one of those demanding payment, don't have any more than a few dollars in any account in any branch of that bank in your name or anyone else's, including your wife, children, or company. Banks are well known for exercising what they like to call their "right of offset," and they frequently don't hesitate to help themselves to any funds in their possession that might even remotely be considered yours. Thus, if the Last National Bank is demanding your tardy car payment, withdraw any money you, your wife, or kids may have there and put it somewhere else. Don't close the account, however. Leave a few dollars in it so the bank won't think you're leaving town.

(2) Never permit someone to repossess collateral without a written order signed by a judge.

(3) Never give a bad check, even if the creditor promises he'll hold it until you tell him it will clear. He won't, and you'll then have the bank after you, and perhaps the local gendarmes as well.

34

(4) Never ignore a summons. See a lawyer.

(5) Never, never mention marital problems.

STEP EIGHT: LEARN TO LIVE WITH LESS

No family magazine today is complete without the obligatory article on "home economizing." If all the money-saving tips that are being published were compiled in a single volume, the cost of printing alone would be sufficient to throw any purchaser into immediate bankruptcy. Go to your local public library, and ask the librarian to help you find recent books and publications containing ideas for saving money.

When you must buy something, be a comparison shopper. Write down on a pad what you need, and then call or visit the appropriate store and jot down the prices they quote you. If you use the telephone, be sure to get the name of the person who quotes you a price. You may need it later.

Contrary to the usual sound practice of buying "quality," you may find that the purchase of cheaper merchandise will be satisfactory for now, and in the present dilemma, a short-term saving is what counts.

Examine your bills, and try to figure out the creditor's billing schedule. For example, if your bills from store X come on the 15 of each month, regardless of when the purchase was made, shop in that store on the 16 or 17. You gain a month of free credit that way.

If you're buying with cash, try to convince the merchant to give you a discount if he permits others to charge on credit cards. There's no reason why you should subsidize his other customers and share the merchant's cost of handling credit cards if you're not using them.

There are, literally, thousands of useful techniques for saving money. Use your library. It can be enormously helpful. But, alas, all the suggestions outlined above may not have worked. You have, no doubt, been diligent, but because of peculiar circumstances weren't able to recover from the disease of overextension. The disease is not fatal, however, and radical financial surgery can cure it most effectively. For details, read the following section.

PERSONAL BANKRUPTCY

CHAPTER NINE

Introduction to Personal Bankruptcy

By paying a nominal fee, filing the correct papers in the right place, giving up certain assets, and making a brief appearance in court, a person's obligation to pay debts—regardless of their amount—can be eliminated. In one sentence, subject to careful qualification in this section of the book, that is what bankruptcy is all about.

In unparalleled numbers, tens of thousands of Americans are now discovering that bankruptcy is neither a curse nor a hassle, but is instead a simple, perfectly legal way to make a fresh financial start. The statistics are mind-boggling.

During the fiscal year of 1976, over a quarter of a million Americans filed for bankruptcy, a figure nearly twice that of previous years. The trend, moreover, is expected to continue, unless Congress puts its legislative foot down by amending the present law to deny bankruptcy relief to large classes of petitioners (see Chapter 14).

Several years ago, six states[1] accounted for more than half the bankruptcy filings in the country. The word has now spread across the land, however, and such "pockets" of bankruptcy filings are disappearing.

[1]California, Ohio, Illinois, Alabama, Tennessee, and Georgia.

39

PERSONAL BANKRUPTCY CASES COMMENCED
FISCAL YEARS 1965–1977

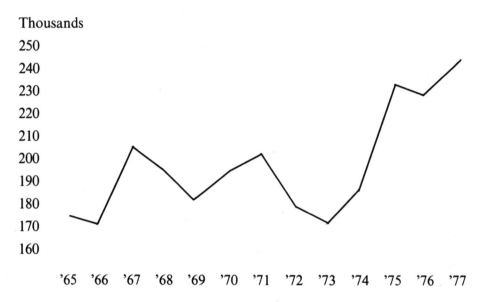

At the onset of any discussion of bankruptcy, several popular myths should be dispelled.

(1) "Bankruptcy destroys your credit rating." Nonsense! The truth is that few petitioners, if any, have much of a credit rating left when they file. It's hard to destroy nothing. Besides, many creditors *prefer* to extend credit to someone recently bankrupt because they know he is one customer who can't declare bankruptcy for a while!

(2) "Bankruptcy imposes restrictions." False, except that declaring bankruptcy restricts you from doing it again within six years. There are absolutely no restrictions as to what business you can go into, how much money you can make, or what you can do with it.

(3) "You must be 'broke enough' to file bankruptcy." No. There is neither a minimum nor a maximum debt limit. In fact, there are some cases on record in which the petitioner's debts were exceeded by his cost of filing! Figure that one out.

(4) "Bankruptcy is for businesses, not people." No, no, no. That it's for ordinary people is a too well kept secret.

40

In short, bankruptcy is a straightforward and honest means of relief from serious financial difficulties. And it stands ready to help *you.*

Where and when it all started, nobody is certain. One of the earliest references to something sounding very much like modern bankruptcy is found in the Bible, Deuteronomy 15:1-2 (Revised Standard Version):

> At the end of every seven years you shall grant a release. And this is the manner of the release: every creditor shall release what he has lent his neighbor; he shall not exact it of his neighbor, his brother, because the Lord's release has been proclaimed.

Thus, while it cannot be said conclusively that bankruptcy has a Biblical *origin,* there is persuasive evidence to rebut the argument that God did not intend man to file bankruptcy since He did not give him forms.

The term *bankruptcy* seems to date back to ancient Italian history to a time when merchants offered their wares from benches on the piazza. When one became insolvent,[2] his bench was broken, and he became known as a *banco-rotto* (broken bench). The French imported the term in the more elegant *banquerotte* and, with some help from the English "bankerout," *bankrupt* appeared on this side of the Atlantic.

In the United States major bankruptcy legislation was enacted in 1800, 1841, 1867, 1898, and 1938. The original bankruptcy law was a device available only to merchants, bankers, and tradespeople, by which they could force into bankruptcy a debtor who had practiced criminal fraud. The 1841 law, however, created the concept of voluntary bankruptcy and made it available to all debtors.

The present bankruptcy law was originally enacted in 1898 and was signed into law by President McKinley on July 1 of that year. Since then it has been amended, revised, and modified many times, the most significant change coming in 1938, in a law popularly known as the Chandler Act.

A glance at the history of American bankruptcy law reveals a rather consistent pull and tug between the interests of creditors and

---

[2]Insolvency is attained when liabilities exceed assets.

the interests of debtors, with an average of 34.5 years between each shift. If this is a pattern, a major tug in the direction of creditors' interests is overdue. The present law is clearly debtor oriented.

Perhaps one of the most frequent mistakes of American debtors—next to revealing marital problems to their creditors—is holding the belief that filing bankruptcy is somehow less than honorable. Nothing could be further from the truth. The fundamental principle of bankruptcy is that when a person has insufficient assets to pay all his debts, what he does own may be divided among his creditors, in proportion to the amount owed each. Short of paying all the debts in full, which is not possible, nothing could be more responsible.

Bankruptcy is hardly a last resort. After all, you could borrow from all your relatives, steal, or simply skip town. But as a petitioner in bankruptcy, you are more far-sighted and realize that with a fresh start, which bankruptcy will give you, you can put yourself once again on your feet and start to practice personal financial management. Moreover, a discharge in bankruptcy does not prohibit you from paying creditors; it simply eliminates the obligation to pay them.

Filing a petition in bankruptcy is *not* an irrevocable act. No one seems to know how many people withdraw their petitions prior to completion, but the number must be substantial, perhaps as high as 10 percent. Moreover, bankruptcies are almost always caused by personal financial emergencies—loss of a job, medical bills, lawsuits, and marital difficulties—and there is certainly nothing dishonorable about losing your job, getting sick, being sued, or divorcing.

Bankruptcy doesn't require any apologies. Extensive research for this book revealed *no* case of a merchant's bankruptcy resulting from the bankruptcy of his customers. And don't think for a minute that the shareholders of Sears believe that none of their credit customers will overextend themselves and turn to bankruptcy for relief.

Finally, consider the effect on you if you *don't* file. The creditors still won't get their money, and your mental, if not physical, health will continue to suffer.

In short, the decision for or against declaring bankruptcy must not be clouded by myth, superstition, or ignorance. You can be forced into bankruptcy, but no one can stop you from filing voluntarily. When you do you'll be surprised that there is no sting and that you're

in remarkably good company. You'll be in the company of enter-
tainers like Mickey Rooney, Eddie Fisher, Vic Damone, Betty
Hutton, and George Sanders. You'll be in the company of many of
the nine out of ten small businesses that fail permanently within their
first five years. Above all, you'll be in the company of the well over
200,000 Americans each year who are finding themselves in financial
difficulty and who realize that, like the Red Cross, bankruptcy
wouldn't be available if there weren't the need and if it wasn't
intended to be used by people like themselves.

CHAPTER TEN

On Lawyers

One of the first decisions you will have to make is whether to hire a lawyer. Lawyers' fees for handling personal bankruptcies range from around $250 to $450 and can go higher. If you've been in business for yourself, and your financial distress is related directly to your business, hire a lawyer. You most likely have *some* assets, and it's better that they be applied to protecting your interests than those of your creditors. In addition, if you own real estate and want to keep it, you should hire a lawyer. Creditors know and expect that a sizable chunk of a bankrupt's remaining assets will go for a lawyer, and they have no grounds to complain. They know you have the right to have the assistance of a lawyer and that the lawyer has a right to be paid for his services.

No law, however, says that you have to hire a lawyer to go through personal bankruptcy. Increasing numbers of petitioners are proceeding *pro se* (for themselves) and are discovering that once they get past filling out the forms, the rest is downhill.

A lawyer does more, however, than simply fill out the forms (which at first glance may be perplexing but, like a Form 1040, aren't so bad once you get into it). He advises you on possible alternatives to bankruptcy (which have been examined earlier in this book), determines whether any of your remaining assets are exempt, and explains the court procedure to you. He will accompany you to court and at all times provide effective blocking between you and everyone else involved in your petition. Perhaps the most important service he performs is seeing that you don't commit any criminal fraud. If you proceed with openness and honesty, however, there's little chance of that.

Nevertheless, if at any time during the bankruptcy proceedings you are formally charged with doing something (or failing to do something) that constitutes fraud, see a lawyer at once! If you don't know one personally, call up several and ask them (or their secretaries) which lawyers in town handle the majority of bankruptcy cases. If the reply is, "We do them—come see us," politely explain that you have some peculiar problems and want a specialist. Another good technique is to call the Clerk of the United States District Court (see Appendix F) and ask for the names of some of the leading bankruptcy lawyers in your community.

To summarize about lawyers: if you can possibly afford one, hire one. If you can't, read on.

CHAPTER ELEVEN

Bankruptcy Law

THE RULES: WHO MAKES THEM

During that hot Philadelphia summer of 1787, which gave birth to the federal Constitution, our forefathers decided to give to Congress the power, in Article I, Section 8, 4:

> To establish a uniform rule of naturalization, and uniform laws on the subject of bankruptcies throughout the United States.

Since they had a lot more important things to do at the time, it took Congress a while to get around to establishing those laws, but they finally did, in 1800. That law has been amended, and today's Bankruptcy Act is the Chandler Act of 1938, with minor revisions. States can pass bankruptcy laws too, but any state laws that are in conflict with the federal (passed by Congress) are superseded by the federal law. And this point is very, very important, because the federal law has large gaps in it that are intended by Congress to be (and are) filled by states' laws. Hence, as far as federal law is concerned, the rules of bankruptcy are uniform, coast to coast. But as to those gaps in the federal law, each state's gap-filling law is

46

different, and therefore the overall laws of bankruptcy are unique in each state.

THE VARIETIES OF BANKRUPTCY

There are fundamentally four types of bankruptcy proceedings, and two entrances into three of them.

First, the entrances:

(1) *Involuntary* bankruptcy. That's what happens when creditors get so disgruntled about your failure to pay that they file a petition *against* you. Obviously, it's a voluntary step on their part, but it's involuntary as far as you're concerned, hence the name. If this happens, hire a lawyer. Don't try to defend yourself in an involuntary bankruptcy proceeding.

(2) *Voluntary* bankruptcy, which is what this part of this book is all about. Despite the pressure being put on you by creditors, you can voluntarily file the petitions, and you can voluntarily get yourself into one of four types of bankruptcy proceedings.

The names for most of the four types of bankruptcy proceedings are derived from their respective sections of the U.S. Bankruptcy Act (Chandler Act).

(1) *Chapter X: Corporate Reorganizations.* This is for businesses that want to work out their financial difficulties without folding up. It's not for you.

(2) *Chapter XI: Arrangements.* Again, strictly for businesses in trouble.

(3) *Straight bankruptcy.* Yes. This is the most commonly used type of bankruptcy proceeding. In it the debtor files his petition, surrenders nonexempt assets, which are divided pro rata among his creditors, and is released from his obligation to pay all but certain debts. Two or three months after he files, he's "adjudged bankrupt" and can immediately begin anew to seek his fortune.

(4) *Chapter XIII: Wage Earners' Plans.* Yes again. This might be for you instead of straight bankruptcy. Imagine a credit counselor (see Chapter 6) with the power of a judge, who can require the creditors to get off your back and accept smaller payments. That's essentially what a Chapter XIII proceeding is. The creditors get *all* their money, but it takes longer. And, if it makes you feel any better, you haven't been "adjudged bankrupt."

A COMPARISON OF CHAPTER XIII AND STRAIGHT BANKRUPTCY

	Chapter XIII		Straight
(1)	Purely voluntary. Nobody can force you into it.	(1)	You can be forced into it by your creditors. But it can also be voluntary and almost always is.
(2)	To be eligible, you must be a "wage earner," i.e., an individual whose principal income is derived from wages, salary, or commissions.	(2)	Anybody in debt can file, regardless of the source of his income, if any.
(3)	Can be filed before, instead of, or after adjudication in straight bankruptcy. You retain the right to declare straight bankruptcy.	(3)	Cannot be filed within six years after adjudication in bankruptcy.
(4)	Filing fee is $30.	(4)	Filing fee is $50.
(5)	Creditors get all their money, over a three-year period.	(5)	Creditors don't get all their money, although they may receive a small portion of it.
(6)	Slightly more involved than straight bankruptcy.	(6)	Relatively quick and simple.
(7)	You retain your assets.	(7)	You must give up nonexempt assets.

Enough background. Now let's look at the details of what you have to do to declare bankruptcy. First we'll look at Chapter XIII proceedings, then turn to straight bankruptcy.

CHAPTER TWELVE

Wage Earners' Plans ("Chapter XIII")

Chapter XIII bankruptcy isn't really bankruptcy. It's a court-enforced plan whereby you make pro rata payments to your creditors, and they stay off your back, by order of the court. What is unique about a wage earner's plan is that it is for people who actually want to pay their debts in full but simply need a little time. The creditors get their money, and you don't have the onus—if you look at it that way—of being adjudged bankrupt.

Until recently, only one out of every six personal bankruptcies was of the Chapter XIII variety. The reason that proportion is so low is generally agreed upon by writers and researchers in this field: lawyers don't like it because (1) it's more work for them, (2) they don't understand it, and (3) it takes too long.

A lawyer's fee for handling a Chapter XIII proceeding should be about the same as for a straight bankruptcy, although he does more work. It is perfectly proper, however, to pay the lawyer a small retainer (say $50) and then pay him the balance of his fee in installments, along with your other creditors who will receive installment payments. Whether he will agree to accept installment payments, however, is something else.

Probably the outstanding disadvantage of a wage earner's plan is that it hangs around your neck for three years. While the success rate for Chapter XIII filings is relatively high (50–60 percent), many of those who do not complete the plan convert to straight bankruptcy—a relatively simple maneuver.

Another complaint frequently made by Chapter XIII petitioners is that they have to pay debts they feel are unjust. You can't pick and choose among creditors in bankruptcy. Either they *all* get fully paid (Chapter XIII), or none gets fully paid (straight).

To file a Chapter XIII petition, you will first need to get a set of forms. You cannot make your own. Forms are generally available at stationery or legal supply stores. If you can't find them, write to:

> Julius Blumberg, Inc.[1]
> 62 White Street
> New York, New York 10013

Ask for one set of S3013 Wage Earner Chapter XIII bankruptcy forms. Enclose a check for $4.25, which includes postage and handling charges. The people there are very fast and courteous and will have your forms in the mail within 48 hours.

During that brief wait, take another look at the list of total liabilities that you worked out before (Chapter 3). Make sure that it's current and includes everybody to whom you owe money, including relatives.

Look at Appendix E, and see how John Doe filled his forms out. They must be neatly typed, and you will deliver or mail an original and two copies to the Clerk of the U.S. District Court for the district in which you have had your principal place of business, have resided, or have had your domicile for the preceding six months. If you are uncertain which district you're in, call the clerk of the nearest one and ask. Be sure to send a check for $15 (you'll pay the other $15 later).

Here are some suggestions for completing the forms, taken directly from the Bankruptcy Act:

(1) *Rule 106.* The caption of every petition shall comply with Rule 904(b). In addition the title of the case as set forth in the caption

---

[1]The forms in this book are reprinted with the permission of Julius Blumberg, Inc., 80 Exchange Plaza, New York, New York 10004, to whom the author is grateful.

shall include the name of the bankrupt and all other names used by him within 6 years before the filing of the petition. If the petition is not filed by the bankrupt, the petitioners shall include such other names according to their best information.

(2) *Rule 904(a). Legibility; Abbreviations.* All pleadings, schedules, and other papers shall be clearly legible. Abbreviations in common use in the English language may be used.

(3) *Rule 904(b). Caption.* Each paper shall contain a caption setting forth the name of the court, the title of the case (your name), the bankruptcy docket number (which will be assigned by the clerk), and a brief designation of the character of the paper (already printed on the form).

"Comment to Rule 614" states the effect of your filing: "(T)he filing of a Chapter XIII petition operates as a stay not only of commencement or continuation of actions or the enforcement of a judgment against the debtors, but also of an act to enforce a lien against his property." Creditors will be notified of this stay when they receive notice that you have filed.

When the petition is filed, the clerk refers it to a judge (called the *referee*), who then calls a meeting of all the creditors named in your petition. At that meeting, which you will attend, the referee will permit the creditors to prove their claims and will ask you a number of questions. He'll want some background on the information in your petition and will want to assure himself that you're not entering into a Chapter XIII proceeding frivolously.

Be sober and contrite. Simply explain that you bought more than you could pay for and suddenly found yourself in over your head. You tried to work out a plan with your creditors but were unsuccessful (see Chapter 7).

The referee then reviews the repayment plan that you have submitted (see Appendix E), and talks it over with the creditors, if they show up. In any event, the referee will have to obtain their written acceptance of the plan. You now pay the additional $15.

When the plan is accepted, the referee will appoint a *trustee* (usually a local lawyer) to administer your plan. The trustee will receive your check every month and will distribute the agreed-upon shares to the creditors, just like the credit counselor did. The trustee will want to have a meeting with you, and it is imperative that you attend.

Rule 13-402 of the Rules of Bankruptcy Procedure prescribes your duties in connection with a Chapter XIII proceeding:

> In addition to performing other duties prescribed by these rules, the debtor shall (1) attend and submit to an examination at the first meeting of creditors and at such other times as ordered by the court; (2) attend at the hearing on confirmation of a plan and the hearing on a complaint objecting to his discharge, if any, and, if called as a witness, testify with respect to the issues raised; (3) if the court directs, file a statement of the executory contracts, including unexpired leases, to which he is a party; (4) cooperate with the trustee in the preparation of an inventory, the examination of proofs of claim, and the administration of the estate; and (5) comply with all orders of the court.

In short, do what the trustee tells you to do. Change your spending and buying habits, and in three years you'll be completely solvent, having never been adjudged bankrupt. A suggestion: don't stop setting aside the amount you've been paying the trustee for the past three years. Write the check as usual, but put it instead into a savings account. Watch it grow.

Chapter XIII, alas, is not for everybody. Many people aren't wage earners, or their income isn't enough to divide among their creditors. Or, perhaps, they don't want to be burdened with payments for the next three years and instead require instant relief. Others may have serious doubts about their liability for debts about which they are continually being hassled. If you're one of these, read the following chapter.

CHAPTER THIRTEEN

Straight Bankruptcy

INTRODUCTION

In a congested nutshell, this is straight bankruptcy: you pay a small fee and file certain papers; you give up certain assets and keep others; the ones you give up are distributed among your creditors; you receive a "discharge"; with a few exceptions, you no longer owe any debts. You are free and have no financial obligations.

Now, for some qualifications and exceptions. Your entire estate can be divided into two categories of assets: (1) exempt assets and (2) nonexempt assets. Sound familiar? It should. Assets that are declared beyond the reach of creditors by your state's law are likewise the same assets you can keep when you declare straight bankruptcy!

Remember that federal law governs bankruptcy. However, also remember that there are certain gaps in the federal law, which are filled by state law. One of these gaps is the determination of what property a debtor need not give up to be divided among his creditors—in other words, what property is exempt.

Assets that are beyond the reach of creditors in a lawsuit are the same assets that you may retain in bankruptcy. Now take another, closer look at Appendix C. It lists the assets that your state legislature

53

has declared to be exempt. Think of these assets as your "black cards": with only them in your hand, you can't lose (see Chapter 4).

If you haven't already, go back now to your inventory of total assets and identify every asset that isn't exempt in your state. Sell nonexempt assets worth more than $30. Be careful, however, to sell them at *fair market value* (see Chapter 3). This is vitally important. If you've transferred anything for less than FMV, you'll be charged with making a fraudulent conveyance, and that could delay your bankruptcy for months, plus get you in trouble. To determine FMV of automobiles, look in a dealer's "blue book" or read the classified ads in a newspaper to see how much money comparable models are bringing.

Stop. Don't sell anything that is *security* (collateral) for an unpaid loan, or an item in which you gave the dealer a "security interest" when you bought it, and you haven't finished paying for it. Cars, appliances, and furniture usually fall into this category. Cameras, clothes, sporting equipment, musical instruments, and tools usually don't. (In most states "tools of your trade" are exempt assets.)

Secured creditors are those creditors who retain a "security interest" in goods you buy on time, or in goods offered as security for a loan. A secured creditor is like a bank holding a mortgage in your real estate: if you don't pay, he can foreclose (repossess). He can do so even if you go bankrupt.

The interrelationship between the law of exemptions and the law of security can be summarized in the chart on page 55.

Of course, once an item is fully paid for, the creditor no longer has a security interest in it, and it is no longer security for a debt (unless you offer it as security for some other debt, like a loan of money).

Your mission, should you decide to accept it, is clear: through a process of selling for FMV and paying secured creditors (unless you don't mind losing the asset that is security), convert as much of your property as possible into nonsecurity, exempt assets. Don't overlook exemptions declared by federal law. They're listed in Chapter 4.

There is one more asset that deserves special attention: life insurance policies. A life insurance policy has a cash surrender value. The more "paid-up" your policy is, the higher the cash surrender value. Whether that cash surrender value is exempt is determined by state law (see Appendix C).

54

If the property is	and it is	
	an exempt asset,	a nonexempt asset,
Security for a debt,	you can keep it only if you continue making payments. Otherwise the creditor can repossess it.	if FMV is more than the balance due, you lose it. If FMV is less than the balance due, you can either (1) keep it and continue making payments, or (2) let the creditor repossess it.
Not security for a debt,	you can keep it.	you lose it.

In states where the cash surrender value is not exempt, however, there is a way to save the policy. Section 70(a)(5) of the Bankruptcy Act provides as follows:

> (W)hen any bankrupt, who is a natural person (not a corporation) shall have any insurance policy which has a cash surrender value payable to himself, his estate, or personal representatives, he may, within thirty days after the cash surrender value has been ascertained and stated to the trustee by the company issuing the same, pay or secure to the trustee the sum so ascertained and stated, and continue to hold, own, and carry such policy free from claims of the creditors participating in the distribution of his estate under the bankruptcy proceedings, otherwise the policy shall pass to the trustee as assets. . . .

If you want to exercise this right, talk to the trustee (more about him later).

NONDISCHARGEABLE DEBTS

Remember "Paul"? He's back again. In Part II Paul represented your most important creditors. Now the reason they were so important should become apparent by the title of this section.

There are certain debts that *not even bankruptcy* will eliminate for you. You cannot legally escape them, even by death. Here they are:

(1) Taxes that became legally due and owing to the United States or to any state or any subdivision thereof within three years preceding bankruptcy, or any taxes due for any year in which you didn't file a proper return, or fraudulently attempted to evade.

(2) Debts you fail to report in the bankruptcy forms. This applies even if you listed the name of the creditor but gave his wrong address. Obviously, you can avoid having a debt held nondischargeable under this provision if you carefully list the creditor's name *and* address. Be sure not only that you have the correct name and address, but also that you list any collection agencies to whom your account has been turned over. If, after a thorough search using reasonable diligence, you can't find the creditor's address, list it as unknown on the forms.

Unless your own lawyer has been bugging you for money, the lawyers who have been writing to you are doing so *on behalf of* creditors or collection agencies. Don't list that lawyer as a creditor; list his client, i.e., the person or business he claims to represent.

(3) Liabilities for obtaining money or property by false pretenses or false representations, or for obtaining money or property on credit or obtaining an extension or renewal of credit in reliance upon a materially false statement in writing respecting your financial condition, made or published or caused to be made or published in any manner whatsoever with intent to deceive.

This one traps more people than you would expect. As you know, when you apply for credit or a loan, you're given a humiliating form to fill out, usually labeled a financial statement. It asks personal questions about everything you owe and own. All too often, the loan officer smilingly pooh-poohs the details, insisting that they need only enough information "to get an idea of your financial picture." Beware! This is the same fellow, no longer smiling, who later appears out of the courtroom woodwork waving your "incomplete" financial statement and demanding that since you "misrepresented" your debt to Aunt Bertha, your debt should not be discharged.

(4) Liabilities for the willful and malicious taking and/or destruction of the property of somebody else. This does not include liabilities for negligence in respect to someone else's person or property (which *would* be dischargeable).

(5) Liabilities that were created by your fraud, embezzlement, misappropriation, or defalcation (stealing) while acting as an officer in any fiduciary capacity. If you suspect you might have problems with this one, see an attorney.

(6) Alimony due or to become due, or money owed for maintenance or support of your wife or child. This applies whether your obligation is based on a divorce or separation agreement, or the common-law liability imposed on a husband and father for the support of his wife and children.

THE FORMS

To obtain a set of straight bankruptcy forms, visit the largest stationer in town, or write:

> Julius Blumberg, Inc.
> 62 White Street
> New York, New York 10013

Ask for one set of S3010 bankruptcy forms, for an Individual Not Engaged in Business. Include your check for $4.25, which includes postage and handling, and your forms will be in your mailbox in a few days.

A complete set of illustrative forms is contained in Appendix F. Be sure that you don't confuse the forms for Chapter XIII proceedings (Wage Earners' Plans in Appendix E) with straight bankruptcy forms (Appendix F). They are quite different. And don't let them frighten you. Bankruptcy forms aren't nearly as formidable as a 1040, and since you're figuring out debts you won't have to pay instead of a debt you owe, they're a lot more satisfying to fill out. You won't need that drink this time.

Use John Doe's forms as a guide for completing yours which,

like his, must be neatly typed. Be especially careful about the following items:

(1) *Your district.* If in doubt consult the Clerk of the U.S. District Court nearest you. Ask which district you're in.

(2) *Names.* Include every name you've ever used during the past six years to identify yourself in business transactions. Don't bother with affectionate nicknames. As long as you're "Poopsie" only to your wife, don't list it. Include your social security number. (Incidentally, *aka* stands for "also known as.")

(3) *Address.* You may list a post office box if you use one instead of a street address.

(4) *Signature.* Don't sign yet. Wait until you can sign in front of a Notary Public, and when you do, sign your full name.

(5) *Verification.* Let the Notary fill out the date of verification, and be sure he or she includes the expiration date of his or her commission, together with a raised seal.

(6) *Statement of affairs* (second page). Fill in the heading as you did on the first page, and simply answer the questions. Under "e," be sure to list any income your spouse may have from which you receive some benefit, even if indirectly. Don't worry if you haven't maintained elaborate books and records for the past two years. Individuals not engaged in business aren't expected to. Don't sign until you are in the presence of the Notary.

(7) *Schedule A: Statement of All Debts of Bankrupt.* Every debt listed on your *Liabilities* inventory should be listed under Schedule A-1 (Creditors Having Priority), Schedule A-2 (Creditors Having Security), or Schedule A-3 (Creditors Having Unsecured Claims Without Priority). Note particularly that both original creditors *and* their collection agencies are listed (with the amount of the agent's claim listed as "duplicate.")

Remember, unless *every one* of your creditors is listed accurately on Schedule A, your debts won't be fully discharged. If you have any questions about the creditor's address, invest some time in making telephone calls to find out. Also, if you have any doubt about whether certain debts are secured or unsecured, ask the creditor. He'll know. If you bought some merchandise on credit and it was later repossessed, but the creditor is demanding a deficiency, he has been converted from a secured creditor to an unsecured creditor through the act of repossession and should now be listed on Schedule A-3.

Don't overlook creditors whose claims you believe are unjust or erroneous. List them, and put down the amount of their claim, despite how you feel about it.

Presumably, you intend to maintain your household utility accounts: electricity, gas, telephone, etc. Thus, do not list the utility companies on your Schedule A. If, however, you have a long-overdue debt from a past account (for telephone service at a previous address, for example), list the company in Schedule A-3.

Does your name appear on any IOUs as a cosigner? Even if the creditor hasn't started coming after you (or the person for whom you cosigned), list him. Therefore, if the friend or relative for whom you cosigned defaults, you'll be immune from a lawsuit by the creditor. Likewise, list the names of anybody who cosigned *for you*. That will protect you against "secondary liability" to that person in the event he comes looking for you after having to pay the creditor.

(8) *Schedule B.* Everything you own must be listed in Schedule B-1, B-2, or B-3. *Everything*. If any of these items are exempt assets (see Appendix C), they must be listed again in Schedule B-4. If you own real estate, you shouldn't be proceeding without a lawyer.

Lump small items into categories, and list the categories: household goods, furniture, carpentry tools, lawn equipment, etc. Remember, "market value" is FMV, i.e., what you could sell the item for now, in its present condition (see Chapter 3).

(9) *Summary of Debts and Property.* Bring forward, from the previous schedules, the totals in each category. Sign in the presence of the Notary.

59

FILING THE PAPERS

Now you're ready to file your papers, i.e., present them formally to the court. Take them and $50 in cash to the Clerk of the U.S. District Court of your district. (The papers can be mailed, but it would be better to file them in person. Someone in the Clerk's office might be able to glance at your papers to see if they appear to be in correct form and will answer any questions you might have.)

File three sets of forms with the Clerk. The fourth copy is for you. The Clerk will now officially notify your creditors that you have filed bankruptcy. The notice will enjoin them from pressing you for payment in or out of court and will tell them the date, time, and place of the "first meeting of creditors."

THE COURT HEARING

The "first meeting of creditors" *is* your court hearing, and it will probably be the only court appearance you will have to make. Theoretically, it is an opportunity for your creditors to get together, ask you questions, and elect someone to administer the distribution of your nonexempt assets to them. In most cases, however, there are no such assets remaining, and the creditors don't even bother to show up.

You, however, are required to attend. In the language of the Bankruptcy Act, you are required to submit to an examination concerning the conducting of your business, the cause of your bankruptcy, your dealings with creditors and other persons, the amount, kind, and whereabouts of your property, and all matters that may affect the administration and settlement of your financial affairs.

Go to the appointed place at the appointed time. Dress neatly, but not flashily (coat and tie for men). Wear no watches, rings, or other jewelry. Bring with you all your financial records for the past two years, together with a copy of your bankruptcy petition. You may want to refer to them. Sit in the back of the room unless directed otherwise, and observe carefully what's happening. Most of the other people in the room will be petitioners like yourself, and by observing them and listening to the questions they are asked, you will be better prepared to testify.

60

When your name is called, sit or stand where the others were asked to, and answer the questions that are asked of you. Answer the questions completely, honestly, and respectfully. Don't, by any means, try to be humorous.

Here are some representative questions and answers:

Q. What is your name and address?
A. *State your name and address.*
Q. Have you prepared these schedules carefully, and are they accurate?
A. Yes, your honor.
Q. Are they complete?
A. Yes, your honor.
Q. How did you get into financial trouble?
A. Your honor, I honestly can't point to a single thing, but it all started when I had an atomobile accident [wife had a baby, house burned down, etc.], and the only way I could keep my job was to borrow money for a new car. Then I got laid off at the plant, and we had to start using our credit cards to live on. One thing led to another, and before we knew it, my wife and I and our two children were in over our heads.
Q. Do you have your financial records?
A. Only our check stubs, a few receipts, and our income tax returns for the past two years.

If, for some reason, the questioning gets heated and threatening, and you feel helpless, ask the judge for a continuance (rescheduling of the hearing at a later time) so that you can hire a lawyer and come back better prepared.

When the questioning is over, the judge will appoint someone, usually a local attorney, to be the trustee of your estate. He will contact you to set up a meeting between you and him. Be sure to attend, and bring your financial records with you. The trustee will also arrange for you to turn over your nonexempt assets to him.

AFTER THE HEARING

When the hearing is over, the danger to watch out for is something called *reaffirmation*. Reaffirmation means that you have dealt with

61

your creditors (to whom your debts were discharged in bankruptcy) in such a way that your obligation to pay that debt is revived.

Creditors may approach you and offer to "help you get a fresh start" by loaning you some money. If they do so, be sure the only promissory note you sign is for the new debt only. Never sign two notes (the second one might be for the old debt). Likewise, never even tell them that you will pay your debt that was discharged. Don't make any new promises for old debts. In fact, if you incur a new loan from an old creditor, to be sure that you're not reaffirming the discharged debt, insert the following language in the new paper you are asked to sign: "I specifically do not waive my defense of discharge in bankruptcy."

A discharge in bankruptcy is not irrevocable. If your trustee or a creditor discovers that you have conducted yourself fraudulently, he can take steps to have your discharge revoked. If this happens, hire a lawyer *at once*.

4
BANKRUPTABILIA

CHAPTER FOURTEEN

Reform: Blowin' in the Wind

Earlier in this book it was pointed out that the present bankruptcy law clearly favors debtors. Largely because of what some people call "abuses," however, a major overhaul of the law in this area is imminent.

One of the so-called abuses in recent years is the growing number of student loans that have been discharged in bankruptcy. Petitioning students and ex-students are said to be abusing the law because they have the *capacity* to earn a good living and to pay their bills, and they have a particular moral duty, if not a legal one, to pay their educational debts. Thus, legislation has been filed in Congress to deny a discharge in bankruptcy to anyone who has the ability or capacity (which an education presumably provides) to pay his bills.

Another suggested reform would make exemptions uniform in all fifty states, change the six-year period to five years, eliminate trustees, and promote the use of Chapter XIII proceedings. A third suggestion would impose a minimum debt limit. This would probably reduce the number of filings but, it seems, would not materially affect the amount of overall debt discharged in bankruptcy.

Finally, some writers have urged that the referee be given authority to convert a straight bankruptcy petition into a Chapter

XIII (Wage Earner Plan) proceeding, and to require a petitioner to undergo financial management training.

Whether any of these specific proposals will be translated into law is not certain. It is safe to say, however, that if the present trend of filings continues, significant reform will come very, very soon.

CHAPTER FIFTEEN

Questions Frequently Asked about Bankruptcy

(1) *Can student loans be discharged in bankruptcy?* Yes. In the past ten years, more than 10,000 students and ex-students have eliminated their obligation to repay educational loans through bankruptcy.

(2) *What is the effect of my bankruptcy discharge on someone who has cosigned a promissory note for me?* He's liable if you don't pay (even if your debt is discharged in bankruptcy), and the creditor can go after him.

(3) *What are the most common causes of personal financial breakdowns?* Personal disaster like accidents, floods, thefts, divorce, unexpected pregnancy, serious medical problems, and loss of a car.

(4) *Can I keep my credit cards after declaring bankruptcy?* No law says you can't, but it's doubtful the companies will let you. Many petitioners report to the judge at the hearing that they have destroyed all their credit cards and thereafter will pay only cash.

(5) *What is the "four-month rule?"* Any transfer of money or property by the petitioner within four months of his filing is

automatically deemed fraudulent if (a) the transfer was made in contemplation of filing bankruptcy, and (b) the transferee knew that the transferor intended to create a *preference* in his favor. *Preference* is defined in Section 60(a) of the Bankruptcy Act as

> a transfer of any of the property [including money] of a debtor to a creditor made by such debtor while insolvent and within four months before the filing of a bankruptcy petition, the effect of which transfer will be to enable such creditor to obtain a greater percentage of his debt than some other creditor of the same class.

Any such money or property would then be recalled into the bankrupt estate to be distributed among all creditors.

(6) *Can a discharge be denied the petitioner?* Yes. If the judge thinks there has been a fraudulent concealment of assets, an untruthful statement in the schedules, or a failure by the petitioner to keep or preserve reasonable financial records, or if the petitioner fails to satisfactorily explain his losses or insolvency, a discharge will be denied.

(7) *Can the $50 filing fee for straight bankruptcy be waived?* No, but the requirement to pay it can be postponed for a short period. Ask the Clerk for details.

(8) *Can a creditor file suit against me after discharge?* Yes, but whether he will win is something else. See a lawyer if this happens.

(9) *What is the most frequently made mistake of bankruptcy petitioners?* Reaffirmation of debts (see Chapter 13).

(10) *Are there any restrictions on the type of business I can go into after bankruptcy?* Not as a matter of law, although some prospective employers may frown on a history of bankruptcy.

(11) *Will I have to give up all my nonexempt assets?* No, the trustee will not require you to give up things that have no market value, like your favorite pipes, fishing lures, and the family cat.

68

(12) *When is the best time to file bankruptcy?* When all moneys due you, including wages, salary, and loans have been paid, and you have received (and spent) your income tax return.

(13) *Do many small petitioners actually get charged with commiting fraud?* No, it's very rare. (But it is a serious charge. *Don't* risk it.)

APPENDICES

APPENDIX A
ASSETS CHECKLIST

Real estate
    Residence
    Business
    Mineral rights
    Easements
Personal property
    Motor vehicles
    Jewelry
    Furs
    Household goods
    Library
    Stamp collection
    Coin collection
    Art objects
    Cash, savings accounts
Securities
    Stocks
    Bonds

Contract rights
    Promissory notes
    Trust deeds
    Mortgages
    Security agreements
    Royalties
    Patents
    Copyrights
    Leases
    Licenses
Insurance
    Life
    Health, accident, disability
    Death benefits from employ-
    ment or fraternal society
Miscellaneous
    Pension, retirement funds
    Income tax refunds
    Furniture
    Tools, equipment, machinery
    Boats

73

Trailers
Animals, livestock
Musical instruments

APPENDIX B
LIABILITIES CHECKLIST

Debts evidenced by promissory notes
Alimony or child support
Mortgage or rent
Utilities
    Electricity
    Gas
    Water
    Heat
    Telephone
Taxes, income
    Federal
    State
    Other
Taxes, real estate
Taxes, automobile excise
Food
Meals away from home
Insurance
    Life
    Health, accident, disability
    Automobile
Transportation
Clothing and shoes
Cleaning and laundry
Medical

Dental
Dues to organizations
Feed for animals
Veterinarian
Vacations
Lawyer's fees
Car repair
Car payment
Books and materials
School tuition and expenses
Entertaining
Church, charitable contributions
Babysitting
Gifts
Household expenses
Physical therapy
Psychotherapy
Home maintenance
Medicines, drugs
Toiletries
Lessons
Cable TV
Allowances
Newspapers and magazines
Haircuts
School lunches
Maid, gardener
Parking fees
Bus, subway fares
Tobacco
Hobbies
Beverages
Recreation
Sports, movie tickets

APPENDIX C
EXEMPT ASSETS BY STATE

Because the law in each state is constantly changing, this list cannot be all-inclusive or permanent. However, the items listed below were on the lawbooks as exempt at the time this book went to press.

In addition to the specific assets that are listed below, most states also exempt income from sources such as employment security benefits, militia pay and allowances, police and firemen's pensions, fraternal society benefits, teachers' retirement benefits, etc. Many states also exempt a certain amount of income received during a restricted period. To determine which, if any, of these payments are exempt, see a lawyer, or ask your local librarian to help you look up the law in the statutes of your state. As a guide for locating additional exemptions, use the references given after each state name below.

There are two important types of property that space limitations do not permit a complete discussion of here. One is *homesteads*, and the other is *cash surrender value of life insurance policies.* The law on both of these varies with each state and is very tricky in some. If you own real estate, you should not be proceeding into straight bankruptcy without a lawyer. If you own a life insurance policy (whether on your life or anybody else's), briefly see a lawyer to determine whether, and to what extent, that value is exempt. He may charge you a few dollars to answer that narrow question, but it will be a good investment.

If you have followed the steps outlined in this book, you should not now own any nonexempt property that has a market value over $30. If you do, you will lose it when you file straight bankruptcy. If you don't want to lose that property, hire a lawyer.

ALABAMA
Code of Alabama, Recompiled 1958, Title 7, Section 629

Cemetery lots, church pews; personal property to the amount of one thousand dollars; all necessary and proper wearing apparel for debtor and family; all family portraits or pictures; all books used in the family.

ALASKA
Alaska Statutes, Section 09.35.080

Books, pictures, and musical instruments belonging to the debtor not to exceed $300 in value; tools, implements, apparatus, motor vehicles, books, office furniture, business files, animals, laboratory, and any other article necessary to enable any person to carry on the trade, occupation, or profession by which that person habitually earns his living to the value of $2500, including sufficient quantity of food to support the animals, if any, for six months; the following property belonging to the debtor and in actual use or kept for use by and for his family: animals, household goods, furniture, and utensils to the value of $1200, including food sufficient to support the animals, if any, for six months, and provisions actually provided for family use and necessary for the support of that person and family for six months.

ARIZONA
Arizona Revised Statutes, Chapter 8, Section 33-1122

Necessary household, table and kitchen furniture belonging to the debtor, including one sewing machine, stove and stove pipe, furniture, carpets, wearing apparel, bedding and bedsteads, hanging pictures, oil paintings and drawings drawn or painted by any member of the family and family portraits and their necessary frames; the family bible, a seat or pew in any house or place of public worship, and a lot in any burial ground; provision actually provided for individual or family use sufficient for three months; fuel necessary for the use of the debtor and his family for six months; tools or implements of a mechanic or artisan necessary to carry out his trade; the notarial seal, records and office furniture of a notary public, the instruments and chest of a surgeon, physician, surveyor, engineer, architect or dentist necessary to the exercise of his profession, with the professional library and necessary office furniture; the professional library of an attorney, judge, minister of the gospel, editor, school teacher and music teacher, and the necessary office furniture; the musical instruments of a music teacher actually used in giving instructions, and the instruments of any musician used by him in the practice of his calling as such; the indices, abstracts, books, papers, maps and office furniture of an abstractor or searcher of records necessary to be used in his profession; the sewing machine and implements of a seamstress actually used in pursuing her vocation; the camping outfit of a prospector in the state, including his mining tools, saddles and burros; the presses, stones, type, cases and other tools and implements used by a person or partnership in printing or publishing a newspaper or in conducting any printing establishment or by any person hired to use them, not exceeding two thousand dollars in value, together with stock in trade not exceeding four thousand dollars in value; two horses or two mules and their harnesses, and one cart or wagon, or one dray or truck, or one coupe, or one hack or carriage for one or two horses or one

76

motor vehicle by the use of which a cartman, drayman, truckman, huckster, hackman, teamster, chauffeur, or other laborer habitually earns his living; one horse with vehicle or harness or other equipments or one motor vehicle, used by a surgeon, physician, constable or clergyman in the legitimate practice of his profession; food for horses or mules specified above for one month; personal items—one watch, one sewing machine, one typewriter, and one bicycle; all arms, uniforms and accoutrements required by law to be kept by any person, and also one gun selected by the debtor; one horse and vehicle belonging to any person who is maimed and crippled, the horse or vehicle being necessary in his business; five milk cows; poultry not exceeding twenty-five dollars in value; the farming utensils and implements of husbandry of the debtor, also two oxen or two horses or two mules and their harness and saddles, one cart or wagon, and feed for such oxen, horses or mules for one month, also all seed, grain, or vegetables actually provided, reserved or on hand for the purposes of planting or sowing at any time within the ensuing six months, and seventy-five bee hives. Also the library and philosophical and chemical or other apparatus belonging to a debtor and used for the instruction of youths in any university, college, seminary of learning or school.

ARKANSAS
Arkansas Statutes, Article 9, Section 1

The personal property of any resident of the state who is not married or the head of a family in specific articles to be selected by such resident, not exceeding in value the sum of two hundred dollars in addition to his or her wearing apparel; the personal property of any resident of the state who is married or the head of a family, in specific articles to be selected by such resident, not exceeding in value the sum of five hundred dollars in addition to his or her wearing apparel, and that of his or her family.

CALIFORNIA
Deerings California Codes, Section 690.1

Necessary household furnishing and appliances and wearing apparel, ordinarily and reasonably necessary to, and personally used by, the debtor and his resident family, including, but not limited to, one piano; one radio and one television receiver; provisions and fuel actually provided for the debtor and his resident family's use, sufficient for three months; one shotgun and one rifle; works of art shall not be exempt unless of or by the debtor and his resident family; one motor vehicle with a value not exceeding five hundred dollars, over and above all liens and encumbrances on such motor vehicle, provided that the value of such motor vehicle, as set forth in established used car price guides customarily used by California automobile dealers, or, if not listed in such guides, fair market value, for a motor vehicle of that year and model, shall not exceed one thousand dollars; one housetrailer or mobilehome in which the debtor, or the family of such debtor, actually resides, of a value not exceeding nine thousand five hundred dollars over and above all liens and encumbrances on that housetrailer or mobilehome, provided neither such debtor nor the spouse of such debtor has an existing homestead as provided by Title 5 (commencing with Section 1237) of Part 4 of Division 2 of the Civil Code. To the maximum aggregate actual cash value of two thousand five hundred dollars, over and above all liens and encumbrances on such items at the time of any levy of attachment or execution thereon, any combination of the following: tools, implements, instruments, uniforms, furnishings, books, equipment, one commercial fishing boat and net, one commercial motor vehicle reasonably necessary to and actually used in a commercial activity, and other personal property ordinarily and reasonably necessary to, and personally owned and used by, the debtor exclusively in the exercise of the trade, calling, or profession by which he earns his livelihood. All prosthetic and orthopedic appliances personally used by the debtor. All lots of land, not exceeding one-quarter of an acre in size, owned, used, or occupied by any person, or by any person in joint tenancy or tenancy in common with any other person or persons, in any graveyard, cemetery, or other place for the sole purpose of burying the dead, together with the railing or fencing enclosing the same, and all gravestones, tombstones, monuments, and other appropriate improvements thereon erected. To the maximum aggregate value of one thousand dollars, any combination of the following: savings deposits in, shares or other accounts in, or shares of stock of, any state or federal savings and loan association; "savings deposits" shall include "investment certificates" and "withdrawable shares" as defined in Section 5061 and 5067 of the Financial Code, respectively. All pews in churches and meetinghouses, used for religious purposes, owned and claimed by any person, or held, in accordance with the rules and regulations of such churches. (*Note:* California has a very liberal and generous homestead law. If you own real estate, see your attorney to insure that you take full advantage of it.)

COLORADO
Colorado Revised Statutes, Section 13-54-102

The necessary wearing apparel of each head of a family, single person, and dependent to the extent of four hundred dollars in value; watches, jewelry, and articles of adornment of each head of a family, single person, and dependent to the extent of one hundred dollars in value; the library, family pictures, and school books of the head of a family and his dependents to the extent of five hundred dollars in value, and of a single person to the extent of two hundred dollars in value—except this paragraph shall not apply to any such property constituting all or part of the stock in trade of the debtor; burial sites, including spaces in mausoleums, to the extent of one site or space for each member of a family and one such site or space for a single person; the household goods owned and used by the head of a family or owned by such head and used by his dependents to the extent of one thousand dollars in value, and owned and used by a single person to the extent of four hundred dollars in value; provisions and fuel on hand for the use or consumption of the head of a family or by the dependents of the head of a family to the extent of three hundred dollars in value, and for the use or consumption of a single person to the extent of one hundred dollars in value; in the case of every head of a family engaged, as his principal occupation, in agriculture or livestock or poultry raising, livestock and poultry not exceeding in the aggregate a value of two thousand dollars, and horses, mules, wagons, carts, machinery, harness, implements, and tools not exceeding in the aggregate a value of one thousand five hundred dollars; and, in the case of a single person so engaged, like exemptions in the aggregate respectively, of one thousand dollars and seven hundred fifty dollars; except that exemptions with respect to any of the property described in this paragraph (g) may not also be claimed under the provisions of either paragraph (i) of this subsection (1) or section 13-54-104.

CONNECTICUT
Connecticut General Statutes Annotated, Title 52, Section 52-351

The property of any one person, his necessary apparel, bedding and household furniture, any arms and military equipment, uniforms or musical instruments owned by any member of the militia for military purposes, any pension moneys received from the United States while in the hands of the pensioner, implements of the debtor's trade, his library not exceeding five hundred dollars in value, one cow not exceeding one hundred and fifty dollars in value, any number of sheep not exceeding ten nor exceeding in all one hundred and fifty dollars in value, two swine and poultry not exceeding twenty-five dollars in value; of the property of any one person having a wife or family, two tons of coal, two hundred pounds of wheat flour, two cords of wood, two tons of hay, five bushels each of potatoes and turnips, ten bushels each of Indian corn and rye or the meal or flour manufactured therefrom; one boat, owned by one person, and used by him in the business of planting or taking oysters or clams, or taking shad, together with the sails, tackle, rigging and implements used in such business, not exceeding in value two hundred dollars; one sewing machine, being the property of any one person using it or having a family.

DELAWARE
Delaware Code Annotated, Chapter 49, Section 10-4902

The family Bible, school books and family library, family pictures, a seat or pew in any church or place of public worship, a lot in any burial ground, all the wearing apparel of the debtor and his family. The tools, implements and fixtures necessary for carrying on his trade or business, not exceeding in value $75 in New Castle and Sussex Counties, and $50 in Kent County. All sewing machines owned and used by seamstresses or private families—this provision shall not apply to persons who keep sewing machines for sale or hire.

DISTRICT OF COLUMBIA
District of Columbia Code, Title 15, Subchapter I, Section 15-501

All wearing apparel provided for all persons within the household, being members of the immediate family of the household, not exceeding $300 per person in value; all beds, bedding, household furniture and furnishings, sewing machines, radios, stoves, cooking utensils, not exceeding $300 in value; provisions for three months' support, whether provided or growing; fuel for three months; mechanics' tools and implements of the debtor's trade or business amounting to $200 in value, with $200 worth of stock or materials for carrying on the business or trade of the debtor; the library, office furniture, and implements of a professional man or artist, not exceeding $300 in value; one horse or mule, one cart, wagon, or dray and harness, or one automobile or motor-controlled vehicle not exceeding $500 in value if used principally by the debtor in his trade or business; all family pictures; and all the family library, not exceeding $400 in value.

FLORIDA
Florida Constitution, Article X, Section 4

Personal property to the value of one thousand dollars.

GEORGIA
Code of Georgia, Chapter 51-13

Fifty acres of land, and five additional acres for each of his or her children under the age of 16 years. This land shall include the dwelling house, if the value of such house and improvements does not exceed the sum of $200:

80

Provided, that none of the above land shall be within the limits of a city, town, or village, and shall not include any cotton or wool factory, saw or grist mill, or any other machinery propelled by water or steam, the value of which exceeds the sum of $200: and Provided also, that such land shall not derive its chief value from other cause than its adaptation to agricultural purposes. Or, in lieu of the above land, real estate in a city, town, or village, not exceeding $500 in value. One farm horse or mule, or in lieu thereof one yoke of oxen. One cow and calf. Ten head of hogs and $50 worth of provisions, and $5 worth additional for each child. Fifty bushels of corn, 1,000 pounds of fodder, one one-horse wagon, one table and a set of chairs sufficient for the use of the family, and household and kitchen furniture not to exceed $150 in value. Beds, bedding, and common bedsteads sufficient for the family. One loom, one spinning wheel, and two pairs of cards, and 100 pounds of lint cotton. Common tools of trade of the debtor and wife. Equipment and arms of a militia soldier, and trooper's horse. Ordinary cooking utensils and table crockery. Wearing apparel for debtor and family. Family Bible, religious works, and schoolbooks. Family portraits. The library of a professional man, in actual practice or business, not exceeding $300 in value, and to be selected by himself. One family sewing machine; this exemption to exist whether person owning said machine is the head of a family or not, and to be good against all debts except for the purchase money.

HAWAII
Revised Statutes of Hawaii, Section 651-66

All necessary household, table, and kitchen furniture, including one sewing machine, crockery, tin, and plated ware, calabashes and mats, family portraits and photographs, and their necessary frames, all wearing apparel, bedding, household linen, and provisions provided for household use sufficient for three months. All farming implements and utensils not exceeding in value the sum of $500; also two oxen, two horses or mules, and their harness; food for such oxen, horses, or mules for one month; one cart, brake, or wagon; and one horse, one set of single harness and one vehicle belonging to any person who is maimed or crippled. The tools or implements of a mechanic or artisan necessary to enable him to carry on his trade; the instruments and chest of a surgeon, physician, surveyor, or dentist, necessary to the exercise of his profession, together with his necessary office furniture and fixtures; the necessary office furniture, fixtures, blanks, stationery, and office equipment of attorneys, judges, ministers of the gospel, and rabbis; the typewriter, one desk and half a dozen chairs of a stenographer or typist; the musical instruments of every teacher of music used by him in giving instruction; one bicycle when same is used by its owner for the purpose of carrying on his regular business or when the same is used for the purpose of transporting the owner to and from his place of business; the fishing nets, dips, and seines, and the boats, with their tackle and equipment, of every fisherman, provided that his means of livelihood is that of fishing. Two horses or mules and their harness, one cart or wagon or stage, one dray or truck, one coupe or hack or carriage for one or two horses, one automobile, one motorcycle or other vehicle, by the use of which a cartman, drayman, truckster, huckster, peddler, hackman, teamster, chauffeur, driver, or other laborer actually earns his living; and two horses and harness and one vehicle, or one automobile or motorcycle used by a physician, surgeon, or minister of the gospel, in the practice of his business or profession; provided that the same shall not be exempt for the purchase price of any goods, wares, merchandise, materials, or the value of any work or labor, furnished for and used in or upon or for any such cart, wagon, dray, truck, coupe, hack, carriage, automobile, motorcycle, or other vehicle. The nautical instruments and wearing apparel of every master, officer, and seaman of any steamship or other vessel. All books, maps, pamphlets, magazines, and manuscripts of every kind, nature, and description, together with the bookcases, shelving, cabinets, and other devices for holding the same; provided, that this paragraph shall not apply to such of the articles herein specified as are kept for sale by any dealer therein.

IDAHO
Idaho Code, Section 11-205

Chairs, tables, desks and books to the value of $200 belonging to the debtor. Necessary household, table and kitchen furniture belonging to the debtor, including one sewing machine in actual use in a family or belonging to a woman, stoves, stovepipe and stove furniture, beds, bedding and bedsteads, not exceeding in value $300; wearing apparel, hanging pictures, oil paintings and drawings, drawn or painted by any member of the family, and family portraits and their necessary frames; provisions actually provided for individual or family use sufficient for 6 months; two cows with their suckling calves and two hogs with their suckling pigs; also poultry not exceeding $150 in value. The farming utensils or implements of husbandry of a farmer not exceeding in value the sum of $300; also motor vehicles not exceeding $200 in value; also four oxen or four horses or four mules, to be selected by the claimant, and their harness, one car or wagon, and food for such oxen, horses, or mules for 6 months; also a water right not to exceed 160 inches of water, used for the irrigation of lands actually cultivated by him; also the crop or crops growing or grown on 50 acres of land, leased, owned or possessed by the person cultivating the same; provided, that in no case shall the amount of crops so exempted exceed the value of $500. Tools or implements of mechanic or artisan necessary to carry on his trade, not exceeding in value the sum of $500; motor vehicles not exceeding $200 in value; the notarial seal and records of a notary public, the instruments and chest of a surgeon, physician, surveyor and dentist, necessary to the exercise of their professions, with their scientific and professional libraries; the law professional libraries and office furniture of attorneys, counselors and judges, and the libraries of ministers of the gospel. The cabin or dwelling of a miner, not exceeding in value the sum of $500; also his sluices, pipes, hose, windlass, derrick, cars, pumps and tools not exceeding in value $200; also one saddle animal and one pack animal together with their saddles and equipments belonging to a miner actually engaged in prospecting, not exceeding in value $250. Two oxen, two horses, or two mules and their harness; and one cart, wagon, dray, or truck, by the use of which a cartman, drayman, truckman, huckster, peddler, hackman, teamster or other laborer habitually earns a living; and one horse with vehicles and harness or other equipments used by a physician, surgeon or minister of the gospel in making his professional visits, with food for such oxen, horses or mules for 6 months. The shares held by the members of a homestead association or building or loan association duly incorporated under the laws of the state of Idaho, not exceeding in value $1000, if the person holding the shares is not the owner of a homestead under the laws of this state. All moneys, benefits, privileges or immunities accruing or in any manner growing out of any life insurance on the life of the debtor to an amount represented by an annual premium not exceeding $250. All arms, uniforms and accoutrements required by law to be kept by any person, also one gun.

ILLINOIS
Revised Statutes of Illinois, Chapter 52, Section 13

The necessary wearing apparel, bible, school books, and family pictures of every person; and for one year after the receipt thereof all money received by any resident of this State as a pension, adjusted or additional compensation or a bonus from the United States Government or from the State of Illinois on account of military or naval service, whether in the actual possession of such person, or deposited or loaned; and $300 worth of property including money, and salary or wages due him to be selected by the debtor, and, in addition, when the debtor is the head of a family and resides with the same, $700 worth of other property, to be selected by the debtor.

INDIANA
Burns Indiana Statutes, Section 2-3501

Real estate, or estates or rights therein or thereto of the value of not more than $700. Tangible personal property to the value of $600. Income or profits of whatever nature of not more than $15 per week. If such income and profits shall exceed the sum of $15 per week, then 90 percent of such income and profits in excess of said sum of $15 per week shall be exempt and 10 percent thereof shall be subject to execution. In no event shall the total of all exempted property exclusive of income or profits under the provisions of this act exceed in value the sum of $1000.

IOWA
Code of Iowa, Section 627.6

All wearing apparel of himself and family kept for actual use and suitable to their condition, and the trunks or other receptacles necessary to contain the same. One musket or rifle and shotgun. All private libraries, family Bibles, portraits, pictures, musical instruments, and paintings not kept for the purpose of sale. A seat or pew occupied by the debtor or his family in any house of public worship. An interest in a public or private burying ground, not exceeding one acre for any defendant. Two cows and two calves. Fifty sheep and the wool therefrom and the materials manufactured from such wool. Six stands of bees. Five hogs, and all pigs under six months. The necessary food for all animals exempt from execution for six months. One bedstead and the necessary bedding for every two in the family. All cloth manufactured by the debtor not exceeding one hundred yards in quantity. Household and kitchen furniture not exceeding $200 in value. All spinning wheels and looms. One sewing machine and other instruments of domestic labor kept for actual use. The necessary provisions and fuel for the use of the family for six months. The proper tools, instruments, or books of the debtor, if a farmer, mechanic, surveyor, professional engineer, architect, clergyman, lawyer, physician, dentist, teacher, or professor. If the debtor is a physician, public officer, farmer, teamster, or other laborer, a team consisting of not more than two horses or mules, or two yoke of cattle, with the proper harnesses and tackle, by the use of which he habitually earns his living, otherwise one horse. If a printer, a printing press and the types, furniture and material necessary for the use of such printing press and a newspaper office connected therewith, not to exceed in all the value of $1200. Poultry to the value of $50. If the debtor is a resident of this state and a woman other than the head of a family, she may hold exempt one sewing machine, and poultry to the value of $50.

KANSAS
Kansas Statutes Annotated, Article 23, Section 60-2304

(a) For the head of a family: The furnishings, equipment and supplies, including food, fuel and clothing, for the family for a period of one year on hand and reasonably necessary at the principal residence of the family. Ornaments of the debtor's person, including jewelry, having a value of not to exceed $500. One means of conveyance regularly used for the transportation of the family or for his transportation to and from his regular place of work. A family burial plot or crypt. The books, documents, furniture, instruments, tools, implements and equipment, the breeding stock, seed grain or growing plants stock, or the other tangible means of production regularly and reasonably necessary in carrying on his profession, trade, business or occupation in an aggregate value not to exceed $5000. (b) For a person other than the head of a family: The personal clothing of debtor. Ornaments of the debtor's person, including jewelry, having a value of not to exceed $500. The books, manuals, tools and instruments necessary to be used by any mechanic, miner, electrician, or other skilled or semiskilled artisan or technician in carrying on his trade or craft, or the library, instruments and office furniture necessarily used by any professional man, in an aggregate value for any such person not to exceed $2000.

KENTUCKY
Kentucky Revised Statutes, Section 427.010

All household furnishings, personal clothing and ornaments not to exceed $1500 in value; tools, equipment and livestock, including poultry, of a person engaged in farming, not exceeding $1500 in value; one motor vehicle and its necessary accessories, including one spare tire, not exceeding in the aggregate $1500 in value, of a person engaged in farming or of a person who uses such motor vehicle in his employment, or traveling to and from his place of employment. The professional library, office equipment, instruments and furnishings of a minister, attorney, physician, surgeon, chiropractor, veterinarian, or dentist, necessary in the practice of such profession, and not exceeding $1000 in value. In addition one motor vehicle with necessary accessories, including one spare tire. The tools, not exceeding $300 in value, of any mechanic, necessary in his trade. One motor vehicle and its necessary accessories, including one spare tire, of a mechanic or other skilled artisan primarily engaged in the replacement, repair, or emergency servicing of essential mechanical, electrical or other equipment in general use.

85

LOUISIANA

No standard exemptions. If you have income from one of the following sources, see your lawyer about exemptions: fraternal society benefits, teachers' retirement benefits, state employees' retirement benefits.

MAINE
Maine Revised Statutes, Article 6, Section 4401

The debtor's apparel; household furniture and goods necessary for himself, wife and children, not exceeding $500 in value, and one bed, bedstead and necessary bedding for each such person, one radio and one television not exceeding $200 in total values and one automobile or truck not exceeding $600 in value. All family portraits, Bibles and school books in actual use in the family; one copy of the statutes of the State, a library not exceeding $150 in value, a watch not exceeding $50 in value and a wedding ring and an engagement ring not exceeding $200 in value. One cooking stove; all iron stoves used exclusively for warming buildings; charcoal, and not exceeding 12 cords of wood, conveyed to his house for the use of himself and his family; all anthracite coal, not exceeding 5 tons; all bituminous coal, not exceeding 50 bushels; $50 worth of lumber, wood or bark; all heating gas, fuel oil and kerosene, not exceeding $200 in value, for use of the debtor and his family for heating and cooking purposes. All produce of farms until harvested; one barrel of flour; 50 bushels of oats; 50 barrels of potatoes; corn and grain necessary for himself and family, not exceeding 30 bushels; all other food provisions raised or bought and necessary for himself and family; and all flax raised on a half acre of land and all articles manufactured therefrom for the use of himself and family. The tools necessary for his trade or occupation, including power tools, materials and stock designed and procured by him and necessary for carrying on his trade or business and intended to be used or wrought therein, not exceeding $500 in value, and one sewing machine, one refrigerator and one washing machine not exceeding $200 each in value for actual use by himself or family; the musical instruments used by him in his profession as a professional musician, not exceeding $200 in value. One pair of working cattle, or instead thereof one pair of mules or one or two horses not exceeding in value $400, and a sufficient quantity of hay to keep them through the season. Domestic fowl not exceeding $100 in value, 2 swine, one cow and one heifer under 3 years old and the calves raised from them until they are one year old, or if he has no oxen, horse or mule, 2 cows, and he may elect the cows or cow and heifer, if he has more than are exempt, 10 sheep and the wool from them and the lambs raised from them until they are one year old, and a sufficient quantity of hay to keep said cattle, sheep and lambs through the winter season. One plough, one cart or truck wagon or one express wagon, one harrow, one yoke with bows, ring and staple, 2 chains, one ox sled and one mowing machine, one corn planter, one potato planter, one cultivator, one horse hoe, one horse rake, one sprayer or duster, one grain harvester and one potato digger. One boat not exceeding 2 tons burden, usually employed in fishing business, belonging wholly to an inhabitant of the State.

MARYLAND
Annotated Code of Maryland, Title II, Section 11-504

Subject to the provisions of S 11-505, $500 in property to be selected by the debtor, but not more than $200 in money. Money payable in the nature of insurance, benefit, or relief in the event of sickness, accident, injury, or death of any person, except that disability income benefits are not exempt if the judgment is for necessaries contracted for after the disability is incurred. Wearing apparel, books, tools, instruments, or appliances necessary for the practice of any trade or profession except those kept for sale or barter.

MASSACHUSETTS
Massachusetts General Laws, Chapter 235, Section 34

The necessary wearing apparel of himself and of his wife and children; one bedstead, bed and the necessary bedding for every two persons of the family; one heating unit used for warming the dwelling house and fuel not exceeding the value of $50 procured and intended for the use of the family. Other household furniture necessary for him and his family, not exceeding $3000 in value. The bibles, school books and library, used by him or his family not exceeding $200 in value. Two cows, 12 sheep, two swine, and four tons of hay. Tools, implements and fixtures necessary for carrying on his trade or business, not exceeding $500 in value. Materials and stock designed and procured by the debtor and necessary for carrying on his trade or business, and intended to be used or wrought therein, not exceeding $500 in value. Provisions necessary and procured and intended for the use of the family, not exceeding $300 in value. One pew occupied by him or his family in a house of public worship; but this provision shall not prevent the sale of a pew for the nonpayment of a tax legally laid thereon. Boats, fishing tackle and nets of fishermen actually used by them in the prosecution of their business, not exceeding $500 in value. The uniform of an officer or soldier in the militia and the arms and accoutrements required by law to be kept by him. Rights of burial and tombs in use as repositories for the dead. One sewing machine, in actual use by each debtor or by his family, not exceeding $200 in value. Share in cooperative associations subject to Chapter 157 not exceeding $100 in value in the aggregate. Estates of homesteads as defined in Chapter 188. Cash, savings deposits in banking institutions, or money owed to him as wages for personal labor or services, not exceeding $80. $500 of any natural person in any account or accounts in a trust company, savings bank, cooperative bank, credit union, national banking association or any other banking institution doing business in the commonwealth.

MICHIGAN
Michigan Compiled Laws, Section 600.6023 (a)

All family pictures, all arms and accoutrements required by law to be kept by any person, all wearing apparel of every person or family, and provisions and fuel for the comfortable subsistence of each householder and his family for 6 months. All household goods, furniture, utensils, books and appliances, not exceeding in value $1000. A seat, pew or slip occupied by the debtor or his family in any house or place of public worship, and all cemeteries, tombs, and rights of burial while in use as repositories of the dead of the debtor's family or kept for burial of himself. To each householder, 10 sheep, 2 cows, 5 swine, 100 hens, 5 roosters and a sufficient quantity of hay and grain, growing or otherwise, for properly keeping such animals and poultry for 6 months. The tools, implements, materials, stock, apparatus, team, vehicle, motor vehicle, horses, harnesses, or other things to enable a person to carry on the profession, trade, occupation or business in which he is principally engaged, not exceeding in value $1000. Any moneys or other benefits paid, provided or allowed to be paid, provided or allowed, by any stock or mutual life or health or casualty insurance company, on account of the disability due to injury or sickness of any insured person, whether such debt or liability of such insured person or beneficiary was incurred before or after the accrual of benefits under the insurance policies and contracts above specified, except that such exemption does not apply to actions to recover for necessities contracted for after the accrual of such benefits. The shares held by any member, being a householder, of any association incorporated under the provisions of Act No. 17 of the Public Acts of 1901, relating to mutual building and loan associations to the amount of $1000 in such shares, at par value, except that such exemption does not apply to any person who has a homestead exempted under the general laws of this state.

88

MINNESOTA
Minnesota Statutes, Section 550.37

The family Bible, library, and musical instruments. A seat or pew in any house or place of public worship and a lot in any burial ground. All wearing apparel, one watch, household furniture, utensils, household appliances, phonographs, radio and television receivers, and foodstuffs of the debtor and his family, not exceeding $3000 in value. Farm machines and implements used in farming operations by a debtor engaged principally in farming, livestock, farm produce, and standing crops, not exceeding $5000 in value. The tools, implements, machines, instruments, office furniture, stock in trade, and library reasonably necessary in the trade, business, or profession of the debtor, not exceeding $5000 in value. The total value of property selected by a debtor pursuant to the preceeding two sections shall not exceed $5000. The library and philosophical and chemical or other apparatus belonging to, and used for the instruction of youth in, any university, college, seminary of learning, or school which is indiscriminately open to the public. All money arising from any claim on account of the destruction of, or damage to, exempt property. All money received by, or payable to, a surviving wife or child from insurance upon the life of a deceased husband or father, not exceeding $10,000. A mobile home, as defined in section 168.011, subdivision 8, which is actually inhabited as a home by the debtor.

MISSISSIPPI
Mississippi Code Annotated, Chapter 3, Section 85-3-1

The tools of a mechanic necessary for carrying on his trade. The agricultural implements of a farmer necessary for two male laborers. The implements of a laborer necessary in his usual employment. The books of a student required for the completion of his education. The wearing apparel of every person. The libraries of all persons including pictures, drawings, and paintings not exceeding $1200 in value; also the instruments of surgeons and dentists, used in their professions, not exceeding $250 in value. The arms and accoutrements of each person of the militia of the state. All globes and maps used by the teachers of schools, academies and colleges. The following property of each head of a family, to be selected by the debtor: 2 work horses or mules, and 1 yoke of oxen; 2 head of cows and calves; 10 head of hogs; 20 head of sheep and goats, each; all poultry; all colts under three years old raised in this state by debtor; 250 bushels of corn; 10 bushels of wheat or rice; 500 pounds of pork, bacon, or other meat; 100 bushels of cotton seed; one wagon, and one buggy or cart, and one set

89

of harness for each business; 500 bundles of fodder and 1000 pounds of hay; 40 gallons of sorghum or molasses or cane syrup; 1000 stalks of sugar cane; one molasses mill and equipment not exceeding $250; 2 bridles and 1 saddle, and 1 side-saddle; 1 sewing machine; household and kitchen furniture not exceeding in value $1200; all family portraits; 1 mower and rake for cutting and gathering hay or grain.

MISSOURI
Missouri Revised Statutes, Section 513.430

(a) For one not the head of a family: the wearing apparel of all persons; the necessary tools and implements of trade of any mechanic, whilst carrying on his trade. (b) For the head of a family: the family bible, family pictures, and school books; all wearing apparel of the family; household furniture not exceeding $200 in value; all provisions as may be on hand for family use, not exceeding $200 in value; 10 head of choice hogs, 10 head of choice sheep, 2 cows and calves, and all necessary farm implements; 2 work animals, and feed for the stock above exempted not exceeding $200 in value; the books of professional men, and the tools or other mechanical instruments or appliances necessary to the practice of any trade, business or profession, and used in the practice thereof; but this subdivision does not apply to any books, tools, mechanical instruments, or appliances kept for sale or barter.

MONTANA
Revised Codes of Montana, Section 93-5813 (9427)

(a) In all cases, all wearing apparel of the debtor and family; also all chairs, tables, desks, and books to the value of $200; and also all necessary household, table, and kitchen furniture of the debtor, including one sewing machine, stoves, stovepipes, and stove furniture, heating apparatus, beds, bedding, and bedsteads, and provisions and fuel provided for individual or family use sufficient for 3 months, and also one horse, saddle, and bridle, 2 cows and their calves, 4 hogs and 50 domestic fowls, and feed for such animals for 3 months, one clock, and all family pictures. An unmarried person who is not the head of a family is not entitled to any of the exemptions herein mentioned, except that of the wearing apparel of the debtor. (b) In addition to the property mentioned in the preceding section, there shall be exempt to all debtors who are married, or who are heads of families, the following property: To a farmer—farming utensils or implements of husbandry, not exceeding in value $600; also, 2 oxen, or 2 horses or mules, and their harness, one cart or wagon, set of sleds, and food for such oxen, horses, cows, or mules for 3 months; also, all seed, grain, or vegetables actually provided, or on hand, for the purpose of planting or sowing the following spring, not exceeding in value the sum of $200. To a mechanic or artisan—tools or implements necessary to carry on his trade. To a surgeon, physician or dentist—the instruments and chest necessary to the exercise of his profession, with his scientific and professional libraries and necessary office furniture. To attorneys at law and ministers of the gospel, etc.—the professional libraries of attorneys, counselors, and judges, and ministers of the gospel, editors, schoolteachers, and music teachers, and their necessary office furniture; also the musical instruments of music teachers; also the notarial seal, records, and office furniture of a notary public. To a miner— his cabin or dwelling, sluices, and pipes, hose, windlass, derricks, cars, pumps, tools, implements, and appliances necessary for carrying on any kind of mining operations, not exceeding in value the aggregate sum of $1000, and one horse or mule with harness, and food for such horse or mule for 3 months, when such horse or mule is used in working his mine or mining claim. To a civil, mining, or mechanical engineer—instruments, tools, books, and records necessary to carry on his profession. To a chemist or assayer—the tools, instruments, and supplies necessary to carry on his profession. To a cartman, hackman, huckster, peddler, teamster, or la- borer—one horse, or mule, and harness for 2 animals, or 2 oxen and harness, and one cart or wagon, one dray or truck, one hack or carriage, by the use of which such person habitually earns his living; and one vehicle and harness or other equipments used by a physician or surgeon or minister of the gospel in making his professional visits, with food for such horse, mule, or oxen for 3 months. All moneys, benefits, privileges, or immunities accruing or in any manner growing out of any life insurance on the life of the debtor, if the annual premiums paid do not exceed $500. All arms, uniforms, and accoutrements required by law to be kept by any person, and also one gun, to be selected by the debtor. (c) In addition to all other exemptions, the following property is exempt, where the debtor is the head of a family, or over 60 years of age: one truck or automobile of the value of not more than $300.

NEBRASKA
Revised Code of Nebraska, Section 25-1556

The family Bible; family pictures, school books and library for the use of the family; a seat or pew in any house or place of public worship; a lot in any burial ground; all necessary wearing apparel of the debtor and his family; all beds, bedsteads and bedding necessary for use of said family; all stoves and appendages put up or kept for the use of the debtor and his family, not to exceed 4; all cooking utensils, and all other household furniture not herein enumerated, to be selected by the debtor, not exceeding in value $100; one cow, 3 hogs, and all pigs under 6 months old, and if the debtor be at the time actually engaged in the business of agriculture, in addition to the above, one yoke of oxen, or a pair of horses, in lieu thereof; 10 sheep, and the wool therefrom, either in the raw material or manufactured into yarn or cloth; the necessary food for the stock mentioned in this section, for the period of 3 months; one wagon, cart or dray, 2 plows and one drag; necessary gearing for the team herein exempted; and other farming implements not exceeding $50 in value; the provisions for the debtor and his family necessary for 6 months' support, either provided or growing, or both, and fuel necessary for 6 months; the tools and instruments of any mechanic, miner or other person, used and kept for the purpose of carrying on his trade or business; the library and implements of any professional man.

NEVADA
Nevada Revised Statutes, Section 21.090

Private libraries not to exceed $500 in value, and all family pictures and keepsakes. Necessary household goods, appliances, furniture, home and yard equipment, not to exceed $1000 in value, belonging to the debtor to be selected by him. Farm trucks, farm stock, farm tools, farm equipment, supplies and seed not to exceed $1500 in value, belonging to the debtor to be selected by him. Professional libraries, office equipment, office supplies not to exceed $1500 in value, and the tools, instruments, and materials used to carry on the trade of the debtor for the support of himself and his family not to exceed $1500 in value. The cabin or dwelling of a miner or prospector, not to exceed $500 in value; also his cars, implements, and appliances necessary for carrying on any mining operations not to exceed $500 in value; also, his mining claim actually worked by him, not exceeding $1000 in value. One vehicle not exceeding $1000 in gross value as established by the debtor. Poultry not exceeding in value $75. All arms, uniforms and accouterments required by law to be kept by any person, and also one gun, to be selected by the debtor.

NEW HAMPSHIRE
New Hampshire Revised Statutes Annotated, Section 511:2

The wearing apparel necessary for the use of the debtor and his family. Comfortable beds, bedsteads and bedding necessary for the debtor, his wife and children. Household furniture to the value of $1000. One cooking stove and the necessary furniture belonging to the same. One sewing machine, kept for use by the debtor or his family. Provisions and fuel to the value of $200. The uniform, arms and equipments of every officer and private in the militia. The Bibles, school books and library of any debtor, used by him or his family, to the value of $400. Tools of his occupation to the value of $600. One hog and one pig, and the pork of the same when slaughtered. Six sheep and the fleeces of the same. One cow; a yoke of oxen or a horse, when required for farming or teaming purposes or other actual use; and hay not exceeding four tons. Domestic fowls not exceeding $150 in value. The debtor's interest in one pew in any meeting-house in which he or his family usually worship. The debtor's interest in one lot or right of burial in any cemetery.

NEW JERSEY
New Jersey Statutes Annotated, Article 4, Section 2A: 17-19

Goods and chattels, shares of stock or interests in any corporation and personal property of every kind, not exceeding in value, exclusive of wearing apparel, $1000, and all wearing apparel the property of a debtor.

NEW MEXICO
New Mexico Statutes, Article 5, Section 24-5-1

The wearing apparel of such person or family; the beds, bedsteads and bedding necessary for the use of the same; one cooking stove and pipe; one stove and pipe used for warming the dwelling, and fuel sufficient for the period of 60 days, actually provided and designed for the use of such person or family. One cow, or if the debtor owns no cow, household furniture to be selected by him or her, not exceeding $40 in value; two swine, or the pork therefrom, or if the debtor owns no swine, household furniture to be selected by him or her not exceeding $15 in value; six sheep, the wool shorn from them, and the cloth or other articles manufactured therefrom, or in lieu thereof, household furniture to be selected by the debtor, not exceeding $20 in value; and sufficient food for such animals for the period of 60 days. The Bibles, hymn books, psalm books, testaments, school and miscellaneous books used in the family, and all family pictures. Provisions actually provided and designed for the use of such person or family, not exceeding $50 in value, to be selected by the debtor, his wife, agent or some member of the family, and other articles of household and kitchen furniture, or either, necessary for such person or family, to be selected as aforesaid, not exceeding $200 in value. One sewing machine, one knitting machine, one gun or pistol, and the tools and implements of the debtor necessary for carrying on his trade or business, whether mechanical or

93

agricultural, to be selected by him or her, not exceeding $150 in value. All articles, specimens, and cabinets of natural history or science, whether animal, vegetable or mineral, except such as may be intended for show or exhibition or for money or pecuniary gain.

NEW YORK
McKinney's Consolidated Laws of New York, Article 52, Section 5205

(a) The following personal property when owned by a woman or house-holder is exempt: all stoves kept for use in the debtor's dwelling house and necessary fuel therefor for 60 days; one sewing machine with its appurtenances; the family bible, family pictures, and school books used by the debtor or in the family; and other books, not exceeding $50 in value, kept and used as part of the family or debtor's library; a seat or pew occupied by the debtor or the family in a place of public worship; domestic animals with the necessary food for those animals for 60 days, provided that the total value of such animals and food does not exceed $450; all necessary food actually provided for the use of the debtor or his family for 60 days; all wearing apparel, household furniture, one mechanical, gas or electric refrigerator, one radio receiver, crockery, tableware and cooking utensils necessary for the debtor and the family; a wedding ring; a watch not exceeding $35 in value; and necessary working tools and implements, including those of a mechanic, farm machinery, team, professional instruments, furniture and library, not exceeding $600 in value, together with the necessary food for the team for 60 days, provided, however, that the articles specified in this paragraph are necessary to the carrying on of the debtor's profession or calling. (b) The following personal property when owned by a male person who is not a householder is exempt: a seat or pew occupied by the debtor in a place of public worship; all wearing apparel necessary for the debtor; a wedding ring; a watch not exceeding $35 in value; and necessary working tools and implements, including those of a mechanic, farm machinery, team, professional instruments, furniture and library, not exceeding $450 in value, together with the necessary food for the team for 60 days, provided, however, that the articles specified in this paragraph are necessary to the carrying on of the debtor's profession or calling. (c) Any property while held in trust for a debtor, where the trust has been created by, or the fund so held in trust has proceeded from, a person other than the debtor.

94

NORTH CAROLINA
Constitution of North Carolina, Article X, Section 1

The personal property of any resident of the State, of a value not less than $500, to be selected by the resident.

NORTH DAKOTA
North Dakota Century Code, Section 28-22-02

(a) All family pictures; a pew or other sitting in any house of worship; a lot or lots in any burial ground; the family Bible and all schoolbooks used by the family and all other books used as a part of the family library not exceeding in value $100; all wearing apparel and clothing of the debtor and his family; the provisions for the debtor and his family necessary for one year's supply, either provided or growing, or both, and fuel necessary for one year; all crops and grain, both threshed and unthreshed, raised by the debtor on not to exceed 160 acres of land on one tract occupied by the debtor, either as owner or tenant, as his home; any house trailer or mobile home occupied as a residence by the debtor or his family. (b) In addition to the exemptions listed above, the head of a family may select from his other personal property, any goods, chattels, merchandise, money, and other personal property not exceeding in value the sum of $1500, which also is exempt. (c) Instead of the exemptions granted in section (b) above, the head of the family may select and choose the following property, which is then exempt: all miscellaneous books and musical instruments for the use of the family not exceeding $500 in value; all household and kitchen furniture, including beds, bedsteads, and bedding used by the debtor and his family, not exceeding $500 in value, and in case the debtor shall own more than $500 worth of such property, he must select therefrom such articles to the value of $500; 100 sheep and their lambs under six months old, and all wool of the same and all cloth or yarn manufactured therefrom, the necessary food for the animals hereinbefore mentioned for one year, either provided or growing, or both, as the debtor may choose, also one wagon, one sleigh, two plows, one harrow and farming utensils, including tackle for teams, not exceeding $300 in value; and the tools and implements of any mechanic, whether a minor or of age, used and kept for the purpose of carrying on his trade or business, and in addition thereto stock in trade not exceeding $200 in value; the library and instruments of any professional person not exceeding $600 in value. (d) A single person, in addition to his wearing apparel, may select from his other personal property, goods, chattels, merchandise, money, or other personal property not exceeding in value the sum of $150, which shall be exempt.

95

OHIO
Ohio Revised Code, Section 2329.62

(a) Exempt assets of every person: wearing apparel to be selected by the debtor not exceeding in value three hundred dollars; the tools and implements of the debtor's trade, or business, including agriculture, to be selected by him, not exceeding three hundred dollars in value; (b) Exempt assets of every person who is the chief support of the family, or who is a person paying alimony, maintenance, or other allowance for the support of a divorced or separated spouse, or for the support of any dependent person, and every widow. The wearing apparel of such person or family, the beds, bedsteads, and bedding for their use, one cooking stove and pipe used for warming and dwelling, and fuel sufficient for a period of 60 days, actually provided and designed for use of such person or family; livestock or household furnishings not exceeding six hundred dollars in value to be selected by the debtor; all books used in the family, and all family pictures; provisions actually provided and designed for the use of such person, or family, not exceeding one hundred and fifty dollars in value, to be selected by the debtor; the tools and implements of the debtor necessary for carrying on his profession, trade, or business, including agriculture, to be selected by him, not exceeding six hundred dollars in value; all articles, specimens, and cabinets of natural history or science, whether animal, vegetable, or mineral, except such as are kept or intended for show or exhibition for money or pecuniary gain.

OKLAHOMA
Oklahoma Statutes, Title 31, Section 1

The following exemptions are available only to homeowners or heads of families: all household and kitchen furniture. Any lot or lots in a cemetery held for the purpose of sepulture. All implements of husbandry used upon the homestead. All tools, apparatus and books belonging to and used in any trade or profession. The family library and all family portraits and pictures, and wearing apparel. Five milk cows and their calves under six months old. One hundred chickens. Two horses and two mules, and one wagon, cart or dray. One carriage or buggy. One gun. Ten hogs. Twenty head of sheep. All saddles, bridles and harness necessary for use of the family. All provisions and forage on hand, or growing for home consumption, and for the use of exempt stock for one year.

OREGON
Oregon Revised Statutes (1953) Section 23.160

Books, pictures and musical instruments owned by any person to the value of $75. Necessary wearing apparel, owned by any person, to the value of $100, and, if such person is a householder, for each member of his family to the value of $50. The tools, implements, apparatus, team, vehicle, harness or library, necessary to enable any person to carry on the trade, occupation or profession by which he habitually earns his living, to the value of $400. Also sufficient quantity of food to support such team, if any, for 60 days. The word "team" in this paragraph does not include more than one yoke of oxen, or a span of horses or mules. The word "vehicle" includes an automobile, truck, trailer, truck and trailer, or other motor vehicle. Poultry and other domestic fowls, kept for family use, or kept for the purpose of raising them for the livelihood of any person, to the value of $50. If owned by a householder, and in actual use, or kept for use by and for his family or when being removed from one habitation to another on a change of residence: ten sheep, with one year's fleece or the yarn or cloth manufactured therefrom; two cows and five swine; food sufficient to support such animals, if any, for three months; household goods, furniture and utensils to the value of $300; provisions actually provided for family use and necessary for the support of such householder and family for six months; also three cords of firewood or one ton of coal. The seat or pew occupied by a householder or his family in a place of public worship.

PENNSYLVANIA
Purdon's Pennsylvania Statutes Annotated, Chapter 4, Section 12-2161, 12-2167, and 12-2168

Property to the value of three hundred dollars, exclusive of all wearing apparel of the debtor and his family, and all bibles and school books in use in the family (which is also exempt); sewing machines of seamstresses, and sewing machines of private families.

RHODE ISLAND

No standard exemptions. If you have income from the following sources, see your lawyer about exemptions: employment security benefits, militia pay and allowances, police and firemen's pensions, public assistance grants.

97

SOUTH CAROLINA
Code of Laws of South Carolina, Chapter 12, Section 34–41

The personal property of the head of the family residing in the State, whether entitled to a homestead exemption or not, to the extent of $500 shall be exempt, and personal property consisting of necessary wearing apparel and tools and implements of trade, not to exceed the value of $300, the property of any person not the head of a family, shall be exempt.

SOUTH DAKOTA
South Dakota Compiled Laws, Section 43-45-2

(a) The property mentioned in this section is absolutely exempt: all family pictures; a pew or other sitting in any house of worship; a lot or lots in any burial ground; the family Bible and all schoolbooks used by the family, and all other books used as a part of the family library, not exceeding in value $200; all wearing apparel and clothing of the debtor and his family; the provisions for the debtor and his family necessary for one year's supply, either provided or growing, or both, and fuel necessary for one year. In addition to the property mentioned in (a) above, the debtor, if the head of a family, may select from all other of his personal property, not absolutely exempt, goods, chattels, merchandise, money, or other personal property not to exceed in the aggregate $1500 in value; and, if a single person, not the head of a family, property as aforesaid of the value of $600, which is also exempt. (c) Instead of the exemptions of personal property granted in (b), the debtor, if the head of a family, may select and choose the following property, which shall be exempt, namely: All miscellaneous books and musical instruments for the use of the family, not exceeding $200 in value. All household and kitchen furniture, including beds, bedsteads, and bedding used by the debtor and his family, not exceeding $200 in value, but in case the debtor shall own more than $200 worth of such property, he must select therefrom such articles to the value of $200, leaving the remainder. Two cows, five swine, two yoke of oxen, or one span of horses or mules, twenty-five sheep and their lambs under 6 months old, and all wool of the same, and all cloth or yarn manufactured therefrom, the necessary food for the animals hereinbefore mentioned for one year, either provided or growing, or both, as the debtor may choose; also one wagon, one sleigh, two plows, one harrow, and farming machinery and utensils, including tackle for teams, not exceeding $1200 in value. The tools and implements of any mechanic, whether a minor or of age, used and kept for the purpose of carrying on his trade or business, and in addition thereto, stock in trade not exceeding $1200 in value. The library and instruments of any professional person, not exceeding $300 in value.

TENNESSEE
Tennessee Code Annotated, Chapter 2, Section 26-201

Personal property to the aggregate value of $1500 is exempt in the hands or possession of a head of family who is a bona fide citizen permanently residing in Tennessee, whether said head of a family be the husband or father, or the mother where the father of husband is dead or has absconded or deserted his family; and such head of family entitled to this exemption without regard to his vocation, or pursuit or to the ownership of his abode. Such head of a family may select for exemption the items of then owned and possessed personal property up to the aggregate value of $1500. Personal property to the aggregate value of $900 is exempt in the hands or possession of a person who is not a head of a family and who is not residing with a head of a family if such person is a bona fide citizen permanently residing in Tennessee, and such a person is entitled to this exemption without regard to his vocation or pursuit or to the ownership of his abode. Such person may select for exemption the items of then owned and possessed personal property up to the aggregate value of $900. Also, there is further exempt to every resident debtor the following specific articles of personality: all necessary and proper wearing apparel for the actual use of himself and family and the trunks or receptacles necessary to contain them, all family portraits and pictures, the family Bible and school books.

TEXAS
Vernon's Texas Civil Statutes, Title 57, Article 3835

Personal property (not to exceed an aggregate fair market value of $15,000 for each single, adult person, not a constituent of a family, or $30,000 for a family) is exempt, if included among the following: furnishings of a home, including family heirlooms, and provisions for consumption. All of the following which are necessary for the family or single, adult person, not a constituent of a family: implements of farming or ranching, tools, equipment, apparatus (including a boat) and books used in any trade or profession; wearing apparel; two firearms and athletic and sporting equipment. Any two of the following categories of means of travel: two animals from the following kinds with a saddle and bridle for each: horses, colts, mules, and donkeys; a bicycle or motorcycle; a wagon, cart, or dray, with harness reasonably necessary for its use; an automobile or station wagon; a truck cab; a camper-truck; a truck; a pickup truck. Livestock and fowl not to exceed the following in number and forage on hand reasonably necessary for their consumption: 5 cows and their calves, one breeding-age bull, 20 hogs, 20 sheep, 20 goats, 50 chickens, 30 turkeys, 30 ducks, 30 geese, 30 guineas. A dog, a cat and other household pets. The cash surrender value of any life insurance policy in force for more than two years to the extent that a member or members of the family of the insured person or a dependent or dependents of a single, adult person, not a constituent of a family, is beneficiary thereof. Current wages for personal services.

UTAH
Utah Code, Chapter 23, Section 78-23

Chairs, tables and desks to the value of $200 and the library belonging to the debtor; also musical instruments in actual use in the family. Necessary household, table and kitchen furniture belonging to the debtor to the value of $300; also laundry equipment, one refrigerator, one stove, and one sewing machine; all family hanging pictures, oil paintings, drawings and portraits, and their necessary frames; all carpets in use; provisions actually provided for individual or family use sufficient for three months; two cows with their suckling calves; two hogs with all suckling pigs; all wearing apparel of every person or family; also all beds or bedding of every person or family; and, if the debtor is the head of a family consisting of five or more members, there shall be a further exemption of two cows and their suckling calves. The farming utensils or implements of husbandry of a farmer not exceeding in value the sum of $300; also two horses or two mules, and their harness, one cart or wagon; also all seed, grain or vegetables actually provided, reserved or on hand for the purpose of planting or sowing at any time within the ensuing six months, not exceeding in value the sum of $200; crops, whether growing or harvested, and the proceeds thereof, not exceeding in value $200. The tools, tool chest and implements of a mechanic or artisan, necessary to carry on his trade, not exceeding in value the sum of $500; the notarial seal and records of a notary public; the instruments and chests of a surgeon, physician, surveyor or dentist, necessary to the exercise of his profession, with his scientific and professional library; the law professional libraries and office furniture of attorneys and judges; the libraries of ministers of the gospel; the typewriting machine of a stenographer, typist, copyist or reporter; and the type, presses and material of a printer or publisher necessary to the pursuit of his business, not exceeding in value the sum of $500. The cabin or dwelling of a miner, not exceeding in value the sum of $500; also his sluices, pipes, hose, windlass, derrick, cars, pumps and tools not exceeding in value $500. Two horses or two mules, and their harness, and a cart or a wagon, dray, or truck, or motor vehicle, by the use of which a cartman, drayman, truckman, huckster, peddler, hackman, teamster, chauffeur or other laborer habitually earns his living; and one vehicle or other equipment used by a physician, surgeon, or minister of the gospel in making his professional visits. All moneys, benefits, privileges or immunities accruing or in any manner growing out of any life insurance, if the annual premiums paid do not exceed $500, and if they exceed that sum, a like exemption shall exist, which shall bear the same proportion to the moneys, benefits, privileges and immunities so accruing or growing out of such insurance that said $500 bears to the whole annual premium paid. All arms, ammunition, uniforms and accouterments required by law to be kept by any person. The necessary food to care for all animals exempt herein for a period of six months, whether such food is provided or growing, or both, as the debtor may elect.

VERMONT
Vermont Statutes Annotated, Chapter 111, Title 12, Section 2740

Such suitable apparel, bedding, tools, arms and articles of household furniture, as may be necessary for sustaining life; one sewing machine kept for use; one cow not exceeding in value $100; the best swine or the meat of one swine; sheep not exceeding in number ten, nor in value $100, and one year's product of such sheep in wool, yarn or cloth; forage sufficient for keeping not exceeding ten sheep, one cow and two oxen or horses, as the debtor may select, through one winter; ten cords of fire wood or five tons of coal; twenty bushels of potatoes; the pistols, side arms and equipment of a soldier in the service of the United States, and kept by him or his heirs as mementoes of his service; growing crops; ten bushels of grain; one barrel of flour; three swarms of bees and their hives with their produce in honey; two hundred pounds of sugar; lettered gravestones; the Bibles and other books used in a family; one pew or slip in a meetinghouse or place of religious worship; live poultry not exceeding in value $10; the professional books and instruments of physicians and dentists to the value of $200; the professional books of clergymen and attorneys at law, to the value of $200; one tool chest kept for use by a mechanic; one yoke of oxen or steers, as the debtor may select; two horses kept and used for team work, and such as the debtor may select in lieu of oxen or steers, but not exceeding in value the sum of $300; one two-horse wagon with whiffletrees and neck yoke or one one-horse wagon used for teaming, or one ox-cart, as the debtor may choose; one sled or one set of traverse sleds, either for oxen or horses, as the debtor may select; two harnesses, two halters, two chains, one plow, and one ox yoke, which, with the oxen or steers or horses which the debtor may select for team work, shall not exceed in value $350.

VIRGINIA
Code of Virginia Chapter 3, Section 34–26

The family Bible. Family pictures, school books, and library for the use of the family. A lot in a burial ground. All necessary wearing apparel of the debtor and his family, all beds, bedsteads and bedding necessary for the use of such family, two dressers or two dressing tables, wardrobes, chifferobes or chests of drawers or a dresser and a dressing table; carpets, rugs, linoleum or other floor covering; and all stoves and appendages put up and kept for use of the family not exceeding three. All cats, dogs, birds, squirrels, rabbits and other pets not kept or raised for sale; one cow and her calf until one year old, one horse, six chairs, six plates, one table, twelve knives, twelve forks, two dozen spoons, twelve dishes, or if the family consists of more than twelve, then a plate, knife, fork and two spoons, and a dish for each member thereof; two basins, one pot, one oven, six pieces of wooden or earthenware; one dining room table, one buffet, china press, one icebox or refrigerator of any construction, one washing machine, one loom and its appurtenances, one kitchen safe or one kitchen cabinet or press, one spinning wheel, one pair of cards, one axe and provisions other than those hereinafter set out of the value of $50; two hoes; fifty bushels of shelled corn, or in lieu thereof, twenty-five bushels of rye or buckwheat; five bushels of wheat, or one barrel of flour; twenty bushels of potatoes, two hundred pounds of bacon or pork, three hogs, fowl not exceeding in value $25, all canned goods, canned fruits, preserved fruits or home-prepared food put up and prepared for use and consumption of the family, $25 in value of forage or hay, one cooking stove and utensils for cooking therewith, one sewing machine, and in case of a mechanic, the tools and utensils of his trade, and in case of an oysterman or fisherman his boat and tackle, not exceeding $750 in value. If the householder be at the time actually engaged in the business of agriculture, there shall also be exempt, while he is so engaged, to be selected by him the following articles, or so many thereof as he may have, to wit: a pair of horses or mules unless he selects or has selected a horse or mule under the preceding section, in which case he shall be entitled to select under this section only one, with the necessary gearing, one wagon or cart, one tractor, not exceeding in value $1000, two plows, one drag, one harvest cradle, one pitchfork, one rake, two iron wedges and fertilizer material not exceeding in value $400.

WASHINGTON
Revised Code of Washington, Chapter 6.16, Section 6.16.020

All wearing apparel of every person and family, but not to exceed $500 in value in furs, jewelry and personal ornaments for any person. All private libraries not to exceed $500, and all family pictures and keepsakes. For each householder, his household goods, appliances, furniture and home and yard equipment, not to exceed $1000 in value; provisions and fuel for the comfortable maintenance of such household and family for three months and other property not to exceed $400 in value, of which not more than $100 in value may consist of cash, bank accounts, savings and loan accounts, stocks, bonds, or other securities. For a farmer, farm trucks, farm stock, farm tools, farm equipment, supplies and seed, not to exceed $1500 in value. For any other person, the tools and instruments and materials used to carry on his trade for the support of himself or family, not to exceed $1500 in value. For a physician, surgeon, attorney, clergyman, or other professional man, his library, office furniture, office equipment and supplies, not to exceed $1500 in value.

WEST VIRGINIA
West Virginia Code of 1961, Article 8, Section 3897

Any husband or parent residing in this State, or the widow, or the infant children of deceased parents, may set apart and hold personal property not exceeding $200 in value to be exempt. Any mechanic, artisan or laborer residing in this State, whether he be a husband or parent, or not, may hold the working tools of his trade or occupation to the value of $50 exempt, provided that in no case shall the exemption allowed any one person exceed $200.

WISCONSIN
Wisconsin Statutes, Section 272.18

The family Bible. Family pictures and school books. The library of the debtor and every part thereof; a seat or pew in any house or place of public worship. All wearing apparel of the debtor and his family; jewelry and other articles of personal adornment not exceeding $400 in value; one television set; one radio; all beds, bedsteads and bedding kept and used for the debtor and his family; all stoves and appendages put up or kept for the use of the debtor and his family; all cooking utensils and all other household furniture not herein enumerated, not exceeding $200 in value; and one gun, rifle or other firearm, not exceeding $50 in value. Eight cows, 10 swine, 50 chickens, 2 horses or 2 mules, one automobile of the debtor not

103

exceeding $1000 in value, 10 sheep, and the wool from the same, either in the raw material or manufactured into yarn or cloth; the necessary food for all the stock mentioned in this section for one year's support, either provided or growing or both, as the debtor may choose; also one wagon, cart or dray, one sleigh, one plow, one drag, one binder, one corn tractor not to exceed in value the sum of $1500, one corn binder, one mower, one springtooth harrow, one disc harrow, one seeder, one hay loader, one corn planter, one set of heavy harness and other farming utensils, also small tools and implements, not exceeding $300 in value. The provisions for the debtor and his family necessary for one year's support, either provided or growing, or both, and fuel necessary for one year. The tools, implements and stock in trade of any mechanic, miner, merchant, trader or other person, used or kept for the purpose of carrying on his trade or business, not exceeding $200 in value. All sewing machines owned by individuals and kept for the use of themselves or families. Printing materials and press or presses used in the business of any printer or publisher to an amount not exceeding $1500 in value; provided that no sum exceeding $400 shall be exempt from execution for payment of wages of laborers or servants for services rendered the defendant. The uniform, arms and equipment of every member of the Wisconsin national guard, and all military property of any company, regiment or brigade thereof. All books, maps, plates and other papers kept or used by any person for the purpose of making abstracts of title to land. The interest owned by any inventor in any invention secured to him by letters of patent of the United States. Cemetery lots owned by individuals and all monuments therein, the coffins and other articles for the burial of any dead person, and the tombstone or monument for his grave by whomsoever purchased. The savings account held by a member of a local savings and loan association as the same as defined in s. 215.01 (23), and the savings account held by a member of a federal savings and loan association organized and existing under the laws of the United States, to the value of $1,000 at the time of the withdrawal thereof (but this subsection shall not apply to any person owning a homestead which is exempt). All defense bonds, war savings bonds, defense stamps, thrift stamps, or savings stamps, held by any person, to the value of $200 in the aggregate.

WYOMING
Wyoming Statutes, Section 1-505

The family Bible, pictures and school books. A lot in any cemetery or burial ground. Furniture, bedding, provisions and such other household articles of any kind or character as the debtor may select, not to exceed in all the value of five hundred dollars. The tools, team and implements, or stock in trade of

104

any mechanic, miner or other person, used and kept for the purpose of carrying on his trade or business, not exceeding in value $300, the library, instruments and implements of any professional man, not exceeding in value $300.

APPENDIX D
SPECIMEN LETTERS TO CREDITORS

132 Elm Street, Apt. 6B
Alto, Kansas 10234

Leverett Furniture
125 Oak Avenue
Alto, Kansas 10234

Gentlemen:

As you know, I am presently behind in my payments to you. I have tried my best to repay my debt and my other creditors, but ever since I got laid off at the plant in December, my wife and I have been barely able to afford the rent and grocery bill.

We have spent many long hours trying to make ends meet on our small unemployment benefits, and we would like to ask your consent to a repayment plan which is realistic, and which we think we will be able to handle.

Our present debt to you is $300.00. With your permission, we will send a check for $12.25 each month, which we believe we can afford. We honestly think that we will be able to keep up with these modest payments, and you will be paid in full in approximately 24 months.

Unless we hear from you to the contrary, we will presume that this plan is acceptable to you. As a demonstration of our good faith, a check for this amount is enclosed with this letter.

My wife and I and our two children are very grateful to you for your patience and confidence in us. Thank you for your understanding.

Very truly yours,

John R Doe

John R. Doe

*   *   *

105

132 Elm St., Apt. 6B
Alto, Kansas 18543
February 1, 1975

Last National Bank
Main Street
Alto, Kansas 18543

Gentlemen:

As you have no doubt gathered from the irregularity of our recent payments, our family is having a very tough time making ends meet. Our youngest child, Jennifer, has recently had to undergo several serious operations, and our medical bills are staggering. They have almost wiped out our hopes of achieving solvency in the near future.

However, we have spent much time going over our budget, and now believe that with your help and the help of our other creditors, we can work ourselves out without declaring bankruptcy, which we have seriously considered, but are morally opposed to.

Specifically, we ask you (1) for a 3-month moratorium against collection efforts so that we can get on our feet again, and (2) thereafter to accept reduced payments. Starting May 1, 1975, we will begin making the following payments:

Creditor	Total Debt	Monthly Payment
Leverett Furniture	$ 300.00	$ 12.25
Linda's Linoleum	210.00	8.57
Master Charge	700.00	28.58
Friendly Finance	2500.00	102.08
Dan's Garage	200.00	8.17
Last National Bank	750.00	30.63
White's Dept. Store	350.00	14.29
Community Hospital	450.00	18.38
Discount Draperies	120.00	4.90
Earl Doe, Sr.	200.00	8.17
Alice's Nursery School	220.00	8.98
Totals	$6000.00	$245.00

Would you please write back and indicate whether this schedule is acceptable to you? Unless all of our creditors accept it, it won't work, and we will be forced to consider more drastic steps.

Thank you very much.

Very truly yours,

John R. Doe

John R. Doe

* * *

132 Elm St., Apt. 6B
Alto, Kansas 17111
March 3, 1975

White's Department Store
200 Main Street
Alto, Kansas 17111

Gentlemen:

I have just received your second collection notice for money due on a washing machine you sold us in November of 1974.

The machine was delivered on November 5. On November 10, having used it several times, it suddenly began to make a terrible clacking noise. We shut it off and called your repair department the next day (November 11), and were told that someone would be out to "look at it." Two weeks and three telephone calls later, a serviceman finally appeared who took one look and listen and announced that he would have to return to the shop for a special tool. He warned us not to use it until it was fixed.

Another week passed with no word from the repairman, and I called a "customer service representative" who promised to "check on it." The next day she called and confirmed that the store indeed had a record of having sold us the machine and that the repairman had been sent out. But she was unable to say when it would be fixed.

Since that time, the only contact I have had with your store has been in the form of rude collection notices.

Please be advised that unless our washing machine is properly repaired by March 15, 1975, I will (1) not pay a penny on the debt, (2) file a formal complaint with the Consumer Protection Division of the Attorney General's office, and (3) file a formal complaint with the Better Business Bureau. Furthermore, I will consider any further attempts at bill collection a breach of my legal rights, and I will take action accordingly. I will not be a victim of pedestrian harassment techniques.

Very truly yours,

John R Doe

John R. Doe

APPENDIX E
SPECIMEN PETITION FOR CHAPTER XIII PROCEEDINGS*

UNITED STATES DISTRICT COURT FOR THE Western   DISTRICT OF Kansas *

In re JOHN ROBERT DOE, a/k/a John R. Doe, J. Robert Doe, J.R. Doe, Jack Doe

Debtor, Soc. Sec. No.   123-45-6789
[Include here all names used by bankrupt within last 6 years.]

BANKRUPTCY NO.

ORIGINAL PETITION
UNDER
CHAPTER XIII

---

1. Petitioner's post-office address is
132 Elm Street, Apartment 6B, Anytown, Kansas 66609

2. Petitioner has his XXXXXXXXXXXXXXXXXXXXXXXXXXXX— *domicile* within this district.

3. *No bankruptcy case initiated on a petition by or against petitioner is now pending.*

4. *Petitioner is qualified to file this petition and is entitled to the benefits of Chapter XIII of the Bankruptcy Act*

5. *Petitioner is insolvent* and *~~/~~unable to pay his debts as they mature.*

6. *A copy of petitioner's proposed plan is attached.*

7. *Petitioner intends to file a plan pursuant to Chapter XIII of the Act.*

Wherefore petitioner prays for relief under Chapter XIII of the Act.

Signed: .... None ....
Attorney for Petitioner

Address: ....

John Robert Doe
John Robert Doe , *Petitioner*
[Petitioner signs if not represented by attorney]

STATE OF Kansas   County of Washington   ss. April 1, 1975

I,   John Robert Doe   the petitioner named in the foregoing petition, do hereby swear that the statements contained therein are true according to the best of my knowledge, information, and belief.

John Robert Doe
John Robert Doe *Petitioner*

Subscribed and sworn to before me on April 1, 1975

Notary
Seal

Mary R. Roe
Mary R. Roe
Notary Public
Official Character
My commission expires 5/11/78.

OF 13-1: Original Petition Under Chapter XIII   Instructions: cross out inapplicable italicized words.   © 1973 BY JULIUS BLUMBERG, INC., 80 EXCHANGE PL., N.Y.C. 10004

*Forms available from the publisher, Julius Blumberg, Inc., 80 Exchange Place, N.Y., N.Y. 10004.

APPENDIX E | SPECIMEN PETITION FOR CHAPTER XIII PROCEEDINGS

UNITED STATES DISTRICT COURT FOR THE Western   DISTRICT OF Kansas *

In re JOHN ROBERT DOE, a/k/a John R. Doe, J. Robert Doe, J.R. Doe, Jack Doe

) BANKRUPTCY NO.

Debtor, Soc. Sec. No. 123-45-6789
[Include here all names used by bankrupt within last 6 years.]

CHAPTER XIII
STATEMENT

[Each question should be answered or the failure to answer explained. If the answer is "None," this should be stated. If additional space is needed for the answer to any question, a separate sheet, properly identified and made a part hereof, should be used and attached.

The term, "original petition," as used in the following questions, shall mean the original petition filed under Rule 13-103 or, if the petition is filed under Rule 13-104 in a pending bankruptcy case, shall mean the bankruptcy petition by or against you which originated the pending bankruptcy case.

This form must be completed in full whether a single or a joint petition is filed. When information is requested for "each" or "either spouse filing a petition" it should be supplied for both when a joint petition is filed.]

1. **Name and residence**

   (a) Give full name: Husband John Robert Doe

                      Wife   Barbara Susan Doe

   (b) Where does each spouse filing a petition now reside?

        (1) Mailing address: Husband 132 Elm St., Apt. 6B
                           Wife

        (2) City or town: Husband Anytown, Kansas 66609
                      Wife

        (3) Telephone number: Husband (913) 987-6543
                        Wife

   (c) What does each spouse filing a petition consider his or her residence, if different from that listed in (b) above?

         Husband same as above

         Wife

2. **Occupation and income**

   (a) Give present occupation of each spouse filing a petition. (If more than one, list all for each spouse filing a petition.)

         Husband Teacher and Chairman of the Social Studies Dept., Anytown
         Wife   High School, Anytown, Kansas

   (b) What is the name, address, and telephone number of present employer (or employers) of each spouse filing a petition? (Include also any identifying badge or card number with employer.)

         Husband Anytown Department of Education
                   400 Main Street
         Wife   Anytown, Kansas 66609
                   (913) 666-9001

   (c) How long has each spouse filing a petition been employed by present employer?

         Husband five years
         Wife

   (d) If either spouse filing a petition has not been employed by present employer for a period of 1 year, state the name of prior employer(s) and nature of employment during that period.

         Husband not applicable

         Wife

   (e) Has either spouse filing a petition operated a business, in partnership or otherwise, during the past 3 years? (If so, give the particulars, including names, dates, and places.)

         Husband No

         Wife

OF 13-5: Chapter XIII Statement

© 1973 BY JULIUS BLUMBERG, INC., 80 EXCHANGE PL., N.Y.C. 10004

*Forms available from the publisher, Julius Blumberg, Inc., 80 Exchange Place, N.Y., N.Y. 10004.

HOW TO GET OUT OF DEBT

(f) Answer the following questions for each spouse whether single or joint petition is filed unless spouses are separated and a single petition is filed:

    (1) Is your current pay period: *Husband*   *Wife*   (not applicable)

        (a) Weekly

        (b) Semi-monthly

        (c) Monthly   X

        (d) Other (specify)

    (2) What are your gross wages, or commission per pay period?   Husband $ 1000.00   Wife $ none

    (3) What are your payroll deductions per pay period for: *Husband*   *Wife*

        (a) Payroll taxes (including social security) $ 100.00 $ none

        (b) Insurance   10.00

        (c) Credit union   none   ----

        (d) Union dues   5.00   ----

        (e) Other (specify) Retirement   35.00   ----

    (4) What is your take-home pay per pay period?   Husband $ 850.00   Wife $ none

    (5) Is your employment subject to seasonal or other change?   Husband no   Wife ----

    (6) What was the amount of your gross income for the last calendar year?   Husband $ 12,000.00   Wife $ none

    (7) Has either of you made any wage assignments or allotments? (If so, indicate which spouse's wage assigned or allotted, the name and address of the person to whom assigned or allotted, and the amount owing, if any, to such person. If allotment or assignment is to a creditor, his claim should also be listed in Item 11a.)

         No.

3. Dependents

(To be answered for each spouse whether single or joint petition is filed unless spouses are separated and a single petition is filed.)

(a) Does either of you pay [or receive] alimony, maintenance, or support?   No.   If so, how much per month?   Not applicable.

For whose support? (Give name, age, and relationship to you.)

     Husband

     Wife

(b) List all other dependents, other than present spouse, not listed in (a) above. (Give name, age, and relationship to you.)

     Husband   John Robert Doe, Jr., 14, son.
                  Maria Elizabeth Doe, 4, daughter.

     Wife   same as above

OF 13-5: Chapter XIII Statement: page 2   © 1973 BY JULIUS BLUMBERG, INC., 80 EXCHANGE PL., N.Y.C. 10004

4. Budget

(a) Give estimated average future monthly income for each spouse whether single or joint petition is filed unless spouses are separated and a single petition is filed.

    (1) Husband's monthly take-home pay $850.00

    (2) Wife's monthly take-home pay .... none

    (3) Other monthly income (specify) .... none

                                                 Total $850.00

(b) Give estimated average future monthly expenses of family (not including debts to be paid under plan), consisting of:

    (1) Rent or home mortgage payment (include lot rental for trailer) Rent $210.00

    (2) Utilities (Electricity $20.00   Heat $35.00   Water $5.00   Telephone $20.00) 60.00

    (3) Food 150.00

    (4) Clothing 25.00

    (5) Laundry and cleaning 10.00

    (6) Newspapers, periodicals, and books (including school books) 10.00

    (7) Medical and drug expenses 50.00

    (8) Insurance (not deducted from wages): (a) Auto $30.00   (b) Other $35.00 (hshld & life) 65.00

    (9) Transportation (not including auto payments to be paid under plan) 15.00

    (10) Recreation 10.00

    (11) Club and union dues (not deducted from wages) .... none

    (12) Taxes (not deducted from wages) .... none

    (13) Alimony, maintenance, or support payments .... none

    (14) Other payments for support of dependents not living at home .... none

    (15) Other (specify) : ....

                                                 Total $605.00

(c) Excess of estim. future monthly income (last line of Item 4(a) above) over estim. future exp. (last line of Item 4(b) above) $245.00

(d) Total amount to be paid each month under plan $245.00

5. Payment of attorney

(a) How much have you agreed to pay or what property have you agreed to transfer to your attorney in connection with this case?

    Not applicable.

(b) How much have you paid or what have you transferred to him?

    Not applicable.

6. Tax refunds

    (To be answered for each spouse whether single or joint petition is filed unless spouses are separated and a single petition is filed.)

    To what tax refunds (income or other), if any, is either of you, or may either of you be, entitled? (Give particulars, including information as to any refunds payable jointly to you or any other person. All such refunds should also be listed in Item 13(b).)

    None (1974 tax refund has been received and spent).

7. Bank accounts and safe deposit boxes

    (To be answered for each spouse whether single or joint petition is filed unless spouses are separated and a single petition is filed.)

(a) Does either of you currently have any bank or savings and loan accounts, checking or savings? (If so, give name and address of bank, nature of account, current balance, and name and address of every other person authorized to make withdrawals from the account. Such accounts should also be listed in Item 13(b).)

    Joint checking account, Last National Bank, Anytown, Kansas, No. 642-711-11. Current balance $32.45. Only petitioner and spouse are authorized to make withdrawals.

    Joint savings account, Elm Street Savings and Loan, Anytown, Kansas, No. 87-643. Current balance $90.00. Only petitioner and spouse are authorized to make withdrawals.

7. Bank accounts and safe deposit boxes (continued)

(b) Does either of you currently keep any safe deposit boxes or other depositories? (If so, give name and address of bank or other depository, name and address of every other person who has a right of access thereto, and a brief description of the contents thereof, which should also be listed in Item 13(b).)

No.

8. Prior Bankruptcy

What proceedings under the Bankruptcy Act have previously been brought by or against either spouse filing a petition? (State the location of the bankruptcy court, the nature and number of each proceeding, the date when it was filed, and whether a discharge was granted or refused, the proceeding was dismissed, or a composition, arrangement, or plan was confirmed.)

None.

9. Foreclosures, executions, and attachments

(To be answered for each spouse whether single or joint petition is filed unless spouses are separated and a single petition is filed.)

(a) Is any of the property of either of you, including real estate, involved in a foreclosure proceeding, in or out of court? (If so, identify the property and the person foreclosing.)

No.

(b) Has any property or income of either of you been attached, garnished, or seized under any legal or equitable process within the 4 months immediately preceding the filing of the original petition herein? (If so, describe the property seized, or person garnished, and at whose suit.)

None.

10. Repossessions and returns

(To be answered for each spouse whether single or joint petition is filed unless spouses are separated and a single petition is filed.)

Has any property of either of you been returned to, repossessed, or seized by the seller or by any other party, including a landlord, during the 4 months immediately preceding the filing of the original petition herein? (If so, give particulars, including the name and address of the party getting the property and its description and value.)

Deep freezer was repossessed by White's Department Store, 200 Main Street, Anytown, Kansas, (seller) on or about March 10, 1975. Balance due on purchase price was $250. White's Dept. Store is claiming a $50.00 deficiency. (value: $200.00).

11. Debts (To be answered for each spouse whether single or joint petition is filed.)

(a) *Secured Debts.*—List all debts which are or may be secured by real or personal property. (Indicate in sixth column, if debt payable in stallments, the amount of each installment, the installment period (monthly, weekly, or other) and number of installments in arrears, if any. Indicate in last column whether husband or wife solely liable, or whether you are jointly liable.)

Creditor's name and address (if unknown, so state)	Consideration or basis for debt	Amount claimed by creditor	If disputed, amount admitted by debtor	Description of collateral (include year and make of automobile)	Installment amount, period, and number of installments in arrears	Husband or wife solely liable, or jointly liable
White's Dept. Store 200 Main Street Anytown, Kansas	washing machine, dryer, freezer (repossessed).	$350.00		Maytag washer & dryer	$25/mo. 5 pmts. in arrs.	joint.
Friendly Finance 18 South Street Anytown, Kansas	loan.	$2500.00		household furnishings	$45/mo. 3 pmts in arrs.	husband solely liable

OF 13-5: Chapter XIII Statement: page 4   © 1973 BY JULIUS BLUMBERG, INC., 80 EXCHANGE PL., N.Y.C. 10004

112

11. Debts (continued)

(b) *Unsecured Debts.*—List all other debts, liquidated and unliquidated, including taxes, attorneys' fees and tort claims.

Creditor's name and address (if unknown, so state)	Consideration or basis for debt	Amount claimed by creditor	If disputed, amount admitted by debtor	Husband or wife solely liable, or jointly liable
Leverett Furniture, 125 Oak Ave., Anytown, Kan.	furniture	$300.00		jointly
Linda's Linoleim, 16 West St., Anytown, Kan.	kit. floor	210.00		hus. sole
Master Charge, 21 East St., Anytown;	misc. goods	700.00		" "
Dan's Garage, 61 Market Road, Anytown, Kan.	car repair	200.00		" "
Last National Bank, Main St., Anytown, Kan.	per. loan	750.00		" "
Community Hospital, Anytown, Kan.	son's appendectomy	450.00		" "
Discount Draperies, P.O. Box 41, Anytown,	draperies	120.00		jointly
Earl Doe, Sr., Input, Kansas,	per. loan.	200.00		hus. sole
Alice's Nursery School Yellow Brick Road, Anytown, Kansas	babysitting/tuition	220.00		jointly

12. Codebtors   (To be answered for each spouse whether single or joint petition is filed.)

(a) Are any other persons liable, as cosigners or in any other manner, on any of the debts of either of you or are either of you so liable on the debts of others? (If so, give particulars, indicating which spouse liable and including names of creditors, nature of debt, names and addresses of codebtors, and their relationship, if any, to you.)

No.

(b) If so, have such codebtors made any payments on such debts? (Give name of each codebtor and amount paid by him.)

No.

(c) Have either of you made any payments on such debts? (If so, specify total amount paid to each creditor, whether paid by husband or wife, and name of codebtor.)

No.

13. Property   (To be answered for each spouse whether single or joint petition is filed.)

(a) *Real Property.*—List all real property owned by either of you at date of filing of original petition herein. (Indicate in last column whether owned solely by husband or wife, or jointly.)

Description and location of property	Name of any co-owner other than spouse	Present market value (without deduction for mortgage or other security interest)	Amount of mortgage or other security interest on this property	Name of mortgagee or other secured creditor	Value claimed exempt, if any	Owned solely by husband or wife, or jointly

None.

13. Property (continued)

(b) *Personal Property.*—List all other property owned by either of you at date of filing of original petition herein.

Description	Location of property if not at debtor's residence	Name of any co-owner other than spouse	Present market value (without deduction for mortgage or other security interest).	Amount of mortgage or other security interest on this property	Name of mortgage or other secured creditor	Value claimed exempt, if any	Owned solely by husband or wife, or jointly
Autos (give year and make):							
1972 Pontiac Ventura			$1100.00	none	none	none	hus.sole
Household goods:							
Maytag Washer			150.00	$300.00	White's		jointly
Maytag Dryer			150.00		Dept. Store		
Furniture			700.00	up to $2500.00 lien to Friendly Finance (section 11)			hus. sole.
Dishes, kitchenware			200.00	none	none		jointly
Linen, other household goods			100.00	none	none		"
Set of encyclopedias		approx.	100.00	none	none		"
Vacuum cleaner		"	35.00	"	"		"
TV, radio, clock		"	165.00	"	"		"
Personal effects:							
Clothing for petitioner and family			unknown	none	none		by each member
personal jewelry		approx.	$25.00	none	none		hus. sole.
wristwatch		"	50.00	"	"		" "
Other (specify):							
one 22 cal. rifle			approx.$35.00	"	"		hus. solely

STATE OF **Kansas**   County of **Washington**   ss: **April 1, 1975**

I, **John Robert Doe** do hereby swear that I have read the answers contained in the foregoing statement, consisting of **7** sheets, and that they are true and complete to the best of my knowledge, information, and belief.

Subscribed and sworn to before me on
April 1, 1975

(Notary Seal)

John Robert Doe
✓John Robert Doe, Petitioner and   *Husband*

Mary R. Roe
Mary R. Roe .... Notary Public
My commission expires 5/11/78.

I, do hereby swear that I have read the answers contained in the foregoing statement, consisting of sheets, and that they are true and complete to the best of my knowledge, information, and belief

Subscribed and sworn to before me on

not applicable ....
Wife

not applicable.

....
official character

Attorney for Debtor(s):
  Name:
   Address:

[To be signed and verified by both spouses when joint petition is filed.]

OF 13-5: Chapter XIII Statement: page 6   © 1973 BY JULIUS BLUMBERG, INC., 80 EXCHANGE PL., N.Y.C. 10004

APPENDIX E | SPECIMEN PETITION FOR CHAPTER XIII PROCEEDINGS

UNITED STATES DISTRICT COURT FOR THE   Western   DISTRICT OF   Kansas* .

In re JOHN ROBERT DOE, a/k/a John R. Doe, J. Robert Doe, J. R. Doe, Jack Doe	BANKRUPTCY NO.
Debtor, Soc. Sec. No. 123-45-6789 [Include here all names used by bankrupt within last 6 years.]	CHAPTER XIII PLAN

1. The future earnings of the debtor are submitted to the supervision and control of the court and the *debtor* ~~XXXXXXXXXXXXXXXX~~ pay to the trustee the sum of $ 245.00 ~~XXXXXXXXXXXXX~~ — *monthly*.

2. From the payments so received, the trustee shall make disbursements as follows:

    (*a*) The priority payments required by Rule 13-309(a).

    (*b*) After the above payments, dividends to secured creditors whose claims are duly proved and allowed as follows:

        Friendly Finance $ 102.08
        18 South Street
        Anytown, Kansas

        White's Dept. Store $14.29
        200 Main Street, Anytown, Kansas

    (*c*) S~~XXXXXXX~~ — *pro rata with* dividends to secured creditors, dividends to unsecured creditors whose claims are duly proved and allowed as follows:

        Leverett Furniture, 125 Oak Ave., Anytown, Kansas $ 12.25
        Linda's Linoleum, 16 West St., Anytown, Kansas   8.57
        Master Charge, 21 East Street, Anytown, Kansas   28.58
        Dan's Garage, 61 Market Road, Anytown, Kansas   8.17
        Last National Bank, Main Street, Anytown, Kansas   30.63
        Community Hospital, Anytown, Kansas   18.38
        Discount Draperies, P.O. Box 41, Anytown, Kansas   4.90
        Earl Doe, Sr., Input, Kansas   8.17
        Alice's Nursery School, Yellow Brick Rd., Anytown,Kan. 8.98

3. The following executory contracts of the debtor are rejected:
        Lease of Elm St. Apartments, Inc., to petitioner, dated August 28, 1974, covering apartment 6B for the period September 1, 1974 to August 31, 1975.

4. Title to the debtor's property shall revest in the debtor *on confirmation of a plan* — ~~XXXXXXXXXXXXXXXXXXXXXXXXXXXXXXXXXXXXXXXXXXXXXXXXXXXXXXXXXXXXXXXXXXX~~

Dated: April 1, 1975

                                        John Robert Doe
                                        John Robert Doe, *Debtor*

                            Acceptances may be mailed to

                            132 Elm St., Apt. 6B

                            Anytown, Kansas 66609
                                    Post Office Address

OF 13-6: Chapter XIII Plan   Instructions: cross out inapplicable italicized words.   © 1973 BY JULIUS BLUMBERG, INC., 80 EXCHANGE PL., N.Y.C. 10004

*Forms available from the publisher, Julius Blumberg, Inc., 80 Exchange Place, N.Y., N.Y. 10004.

115

HOW TO GET OUT OF DEBT

UNITED STATES DISTRICT COURT FOR THE Western   DISTRICT OF Kansas*

In re JOHN ROBERT DOE, a/k/a John R. Doe, J. Robert
Doe, J.R. Doe, Jack Doe

BANKRUPTCY NO.

STATEMENT

Pursuant to Rule 219(b)

Bankrupt

Include here all names used by bankrupt within last 6 years.

The undersigned, pursuant to Rule 219 (b), Rules of Bankruptcy Procedure, states that the compensation paid or promised by the bankrupt(s), to the undersigned, is as follows:

For legal services rendered (including spouse if both file), Bankrupt agreed to pay .... $ none

Prior to the filing of this Statement, Bankrupt (and spouse if applicable) has paid the undersigned .... $ none

Balance due .... $ none

The filing fee has— ~~has not~~ been paid.

The services rendered or to be rendered include the following:

(a) Analysis of the financial situation, and rendering advice and assistance to the client in determining whether to file a petition under the Bankruptcy Act.

(b) Preparation and filing of the petition, schedules of assets and liabilities, and statement of affairs.

(c) Representation of the client at the first meeting of creditors.

The undersigned further states that the source of monies paid by the Bankrupt(s) to the undersigned was and is, earnings, wages and compensation for services performed, and

The undersigned further states that the undersigned has not shared, or agreed to share with any other person, other than with members of undersigned's law firm, any compensation, except as herein after set forth.

Dated:

Respectfully submitted,

.... not applicable ....
Attorney for Petitioner

Address

....

....

T 1048—Statement of compensation: Rule 219(b)   © 1973 BY JULIUS BLUMBERG, INC., 80 EXCHANGE PL., N.Y.C. 10004

*Forms available from the publisher, Julius Blumberg, Inc., 80 Exchange Place, N.Y., N.Y. 10004.

UNITED STATES DISTRICT COURT FOR THE   Western   DISTRICT OF   Kansas*

In re JOHN ROBERT DOE, a/k/a John R. Doe, J. Robert   ⟩ *BANKRUPTCY NO.*
Doe, J.R. Doe, Jack Doe

                                                    Bankrupt

Include here all names used by bankrupt within last 6 years.   LIST OF CREDITORS

Alice's Nursery School Yellow Brick Road Anytown, Kansas 66609	White's Dept. Store 200 Main Street Anytown, Kansas 66609
Community Hospital Anytown, Kansas 66609	
Dan's Garage 61 Market Road Anytown, Kansas 66609	
Discount Draperies P.O. Box 41 Anytown, Kansas 66609	
Earl Doe, Sr. Input, Kansas 66528	
Friendly Finance 18 South Street Anytown, Kansas 66609	
Last National Bank Main Street Anytown, Kansas 66609	
Leverett Furniture 125 Oak Ave. Anytown, Kansas 66609	
Linda's Linoleum 16 West Street Anytown, Kansas 66609	
Master Charge 21 East Street Anytown, Kansas 66609	

S 1051—Creditors List   © 1973 BY JULIUS BLUMBERG, INC., 80 EXCHANGE PL., N.Y.C. 10004

*Forms available from the publisher, Julius Blumberg, Inc., 80 Exchange Place, N.Y., N.Y. 10004.

APPENDIX F
SPECIMEN PETITION FOR
STRAIGHT BANKRUPTCY PROCEEDINGS

UNITED STATES DISTRICT COURT FOR THE   Western   DISTRICT OF Pennsylvannia*

In re   JOHN ROBERT DOE, a/k/a John R. Doe, J.
        Robert Doe, J.R. Doe, Jack Doe

                                                           BANKRUPTCY NO.

        Social Security#   123-45-6789   Bankrupt

Include here all names used by bankrupt within last 6 years.

VOLUNTARY PETITION

1. Petitioner's post-office address is
   132 Elm Street, Apt. 6B, Alto, Penn. 17111

2. Petitioner has[1] had his domicile within this district for the preceding
   six months (or for a longer portion of the preceding six months
   than in any other district).

3. Petitioner is qualified to file this petition and is entitled to the benefits of the Bankruptcy Act as a voluntary
bankrupt.

Wherefore petitioner prays for relief as a voluntary bankrupt under the Act.

Signed: *John Robert Doe*

☐ Attorney for Petitioner   ☐ Petitioner
(Petitioner signs if not represented by attorney.)

Address: 132 Elm St., Apt. 6B

         Alto, Penn. 17111

VERIFICATION

State of Pennsylvannia   County of   Lincoln   ss.:   April 2, 1975

INDIVIDUAL: I John Robert Doe,   the petitioner named in the foregoing petition, do hereby
swear that the statements contained therein are true according to the best of my knowledge, information, and belief.

~~CORPORATION: I the~~
~~xxxxxxxxx swear that the statements contained therein are true according to the best of my knowledge, information, and belief,~~
~~and that the filing of this petition on behalf of the corporation has been authorized.~~

~~PARTNERSHIP: I a member~~
~~xxxxxxxxxxxxxxxxxxxxxxxxxxxxxxxxxxxxxxxxxxxxxxxxxxxxxxxxxxxxxxxxxxxxxxxxxxx~~
~~xxxxxxxxxxxxxxxxxxxxxxxxxxxxxxxxxxxxxxxxxxxxxxxxxxxxxxxxxxxxxxxxxxxxxxxxxx~~
~~xxxxxxxxxxxxxxxxxxxxxxxxxxxxxxxxxx~~

Subscribed and sworn to before me on
April 2, 1975

(Notary Seal)

John Robert Doe.
                                    Petitioner

Mary R. Roe
Mary R. Roe, Notary Public
My commission expires 5/11/78.
                                    Official Character

OF 1, 4 & 5: Petition for voluntary bankruptcy: verifications

© 1973 BY JULIUS BLUMBERG, INC., 80 EXCHANGE PL., N.Y.C. 10004

[1] Insert appropriate allegations — resided [or has had his domicile or has had his principal place of business] within this district for the preceding
6 months [or for a longer portion of the preceding 6 months than in any other district].
[2] Insert president or other officer or an authorized agent of the corporation named as petitioner in the foregoing petition.

*Forms available from the publisher, Julius Blumberg, Inc., 80 Exchange
Place, N.Y., N.Y. 10004.

UNITED STATES DISTRICT COURT FOR THE Western   DISTRICT OF   Pennsylvannia*

In re JOHN ROBERT DOE, a/k/a John R. Doe, J.
  Robert Doe, J.R. Doe, Jack Doe

   SSN 123-45-6789   Bankrupt
Include here all names used by bankrupt within last 6 years.

BANKRUPTCY NO.

STATEMENT OF AFFAIRS
FOR BANKRUPT
NOT ENGAGED IN BUSINESS

Each question should be answered or the failure to answer explained. If the answer is "none," this should be stated. If additional space is needed for the answer to any question, a separate sheet, properly identified, and made a part hereof, should be used and attached.
 The term "original petition," as used in the following questions, shall mean the petition filed under Bankruptcy Rule 103, 104 or 106.

1. Name and residence.
 a. What is your full name and social security number?
 b. Have you used, or been known by, any other names within the 6 years immediately preceding the filing of the original petition herein?
(If so, give particulars.)
 c. Where do you now reside?
 d. Where else have you resided during the 6 years immediately preceding the filing of the original petition herein?

John Robert Doe, SSN 123-45-6789
Yes: John R. Doe, J. Robert Doe, J.R. Doe,
and Jack Doe

132 Elm Street, Apt. 6B, Alto, Penn. 17111
1942 San Raphael, Los Angeles, California

2. Occupation and income.
 a. What is your occupation?
 b. Where are you now employed?
(Give the name and address of your employer, or the address at which you carry on your trade or profession, and the length of time you have been so employed.)
 c. Have you been in a partnership with anyone, or engaged in any business during the 6 years immediately preceding the filing of the original petition herein?
(If so, give particulars, including names, dates, and places.)
 d. What amount of income have you received from your trade or profession during each of the 2 calendar years immediately preceding the filing of the original petition herein?
 e. What amount of income have you received from other sources during each of these 2 years?
(Give particulars, including each source, and the amount received therefrom.)

Teacher and Chairman of the Social Studies Dept.,
Alto High School, Alto, Penn. 5 years as
teacher, 2 as Chairman.
No.

1974:$12,000 (gross)
1973:$10,500 (gross)

1974: wife contributed $4,300 to family budget
1973: "   " $3,200 " "   "

3. Tax returns and refunds.
 a. Where did you file your last federal and state income tax returns for the 2 years immediately preceding the filing of the original petition herein?
 b. What tax refunds (income and other) have you received during the year immediately preceding the filing of the original petition herein?
 c. To what tax refunds (income or other), if any, are you, or may you be, entitled?
(Give particulars, including information as to any refund payable jointly to you and your spouse or any other person.)

Federal: Philadelphia, Penn.
State: Pittsburgh, Penn.

Federal: $230; State: $170.

unknown

4. Bank accounts and safe deposit boxes.
 a. What bank accounts have you maintained alone or together with any other person, and in your own or any other name within the 2 years immediately preceding the filing of the original petition herein?
(Give the name and address of each bank, the name in which the deposit was maintained, and the name and address of every other person authorized to make withdrawals from such account.)
 b. What safe deposit box or boxes or other depository or depositories have you kept or used for your securities, cash, or other valuables within the 2 years immediately preceding the filing of the original petition herein?
(Give the name and address of the bank or other depository, the name in which each box or other depository was kept, the name and address of every other person who had the right of access thereto, a brief description of the contents thereof, and, if the box has been surrendered, state when surrendered, or, if transferred, when transferred, and the name and address of the transferee.)

Joint checking account, Last National Bank,
Alto, Penn. Only petitioner and spouse authorized to make withdrawals. Account in name of
"John and Susan Doe."

None.

5. Books and records.
 a. Have you kept books of account or records relating to your affairs within the 2 years immediately preceding the filing of the original petition herein?
 b. In whose possession are these books or records?
(Give names and addresses.)
 c. If any of these books or records are not available, explain.
 d. Have any books of account or records relating to your affairs been destroyed, lost or otherwise disposed of within the 2 years immediately preceding the filing of the original petition herein?
(If so, give particulars, including date of destruction, loss, or disposition, and reason therefor.)

No, except for check stubs.

John Robert Doe, (petitioner) 132 Elm Street
Apt. 6B, Alto, Penn.

No.

6. Property held for another person.
 What property do you hold for any other person?
(Give name and address of each person, and describe the property, or value thereof, and all writings relating thereto.)

None.

7. Prior bankruptcy.
 What proceedings under the Bankruptcy Act have previously been brought by or against you?
(State the location of the bankruptcy court, the nature and number of each proceeding, the date when it was filed, and whether a discharge was granted or refused, the proceeding was dismissed, or a composition, arrangement, or plan was confirmed.)

None.

OF 7 statement of affairs: not engaged in business: page 1

*Forms available from the publisher, Julius Blumberg, Inc., 80 Exchange Place, N.Y., N.Y. 10004.

8. Receiverships, general assignments, and other modes of liquidation.

a. Was any of your property, at the time of the filing of the original petition herein, in the hands of a receiver, trustee, or other liquidating agent?
(If so, give a brief description of the property, the name and address of the receiver, trustee, or other agent, and, if the agent was appointed in a court proceeding, the name and location of the court and the nature of the proceeding.)

No.

b. Have you made any assignment of your property for the benefit of your creditors, or any general settlement with your creditors, within one year immediately preceding the filing of the original petition herein?
(If so, give dates, the name and address of the assignee, and a brief statement of the terms of assignment or settlement.)

No.

9. Property in hands of third person.

Is any other person holding anything of value in which you have an interest?
(Give name and address, location and description of the property, and circumstances of the holding.)

No.

10. Suits, executions, and attachments.

a. Were you a party to any suit pending at the time of the filing of the original petition herein?
(If so, give the name and location of the court and the title and nature of the proceeding.)

No.

b. Were you a party to any suit terminated within the year immediately preceding the filing of the original petition herein?
(If so, give the name and location of the court, the title and nature of the proceeding, and the result.)

Yes:
White's Department Store, Inc., vs. petitioner, District Court of Lincoln County, Docket No. 62785. Action for money owed, judgment for plaintiff. Satisfied.

c. Has any of your property been attached, garnished, or seized under any legal or equitable process within the 4 months immediately preceding the filing of the original petition herein?
(If so, describe the property seized or person garnished, and at whose suit.)

11. Loans repaid.

What repayments on loans in whole or in part have you made during the year immediately preceding the filing of the original petition herein?
(Give the name and address of the lender, the amount of the loan and when received, the amounts and dates of payments and, if the lender is a relative, the relationship.)

Partially re-paid uncle, Earl Doe, Sr., on December 1 and 15, 1974. Original loan Nov. 1, 1974. Have additionally made payments to White's Dept. Store, Community Hospital, and Friendly Finance.

12. Transfers of property.

a. Have you made any gifts, other than ordinary and usual presents to family members and charitable donations, during the year immediately preceding the filing of the original petition herein?
(If so, give names and addresses of donees and dates, description, and value of gifts.)

No.

b. Have you made any other transfer, absolute or for the purpose of security, or any other disposition, of real or tangible personal property during the year immediately and preceding the filing of the original petition herein?
(Give a description of the property, the date of the transfer or disposition, to whom transferred or how disposed of, and, if the transferee is a relative, the relationship, the consideration, if any, received therefor, and the disposition of such consideration.)

Sold set of golf clubs for $100.00 on 12-20-74, to one Fred S. Smith, a stranger. Proceeds applied to household debts and Christmas expenses.

13. Repossessions and returns.

Has any property been returned to, or repossessed by, the seller or by a secured party during the year immediately preceding the filing of the original petition herein?
(If so, give particulars including the name and address of the party getting the property and its description and value.)

Deep freeze was repossessed by White's Dept. Store on or about March 10, 1975. White's address is 200 Main Street, Alto, Penn. Value: $200.00, approximately.

14. Losses.

a. Have you suffered any losses from fire, theft, or gambling during the year immediately preceding or since the filing of the original petition herein?
(If so, give particulars, including dates, names, and places, and the amounts of money or value and general description of property lost.)

No.

b. Was the loss covered in whole or part by insurance?
(If so, give particulars.)

Not applicable.

15. Payments or transfers to attorneys.

a. Have you consulted an attorney during the year immediately preceding or since the filing of the original petition herein?
(Give date, name, and address.)

Yes. Consulted Atty. Peter Hayes, 100 Financial Center, Philadelphia, Penn. on or about 11-15-74.

b. Have you during the year immediately preceding or since the filing of the original petition herein paid any money or transferred any property to the attorney or to any other person on his behalf?
(If so, give particulars, including amount paid or value of property transferred and date of payment or transfer.)

Yes. Paid Atty. Peter Hayes $25,00 for consultation.

c. Have you, either during the year immediately preceding or since the filing of the original petition herein, agreed to pay any money or transfer any property to an attorney at law, or to any other person on his behalf?
(If so, give particulars, including amount and terms of obligation.)

No.

State of **Penn.** County of **Lincoln** ss.:

I, **John Robert Doe** do hereby swear that I have read the answers contained in the foregoing statement of affairs and that they are true and complete to the best of my knowledge, information, and belief.

Subscribed and sworn to before me on **April 1, 1975**

(Notary Seal)

John Robert Doe
Bankrupt

Mary R. Roe
Mary R. Roe, Notary Public
My commission expires 5-11-78.

OF 7   statement of affairs: not engaged in business: page 2

© 1973 BY JULIUS BLUMBERG, INC., 80 EXCHANGE PL., N.Y.C. 10004

Schedule A-2 — Creditors Holding Security *

Name of creditor and residence or place of business (if unknown, so state); zip codes recommended	Description of security and date when obtained by creditor	Specify when claim was incurred and the consideration therefor; when claim is contingent, unliquidated, disputed, subject to setoff, evidenced by a judgment, negotiable instrument, or other writing, or incurred as partner or joint contractor, so indicate; specify name of any partner or joint contractor on any debt	Market value		Amount of claim without deduction of value of security	
			$		$	
Friendly Finance 18 South Street Alto, Pennsylvannia 17111	Security interest in "household goods" given as collateral for personal loan received November 1, 1974.		Approx. 700	00	2500	00
White's Dept. Store 200 Main Street Tenor, Pennsylvannia 19222	Security interest in washer and dryer, purchased in June, 1974.		300	00	350	00
		Total	1000	00	2850	00

Schedule A-3 — Creditors Having Unsecured Claims Without Priority

Name of creditor (including last known holder of any negotiable instrument) and residence or place of business (if unknown, so state); zip codes recommended	Specify when caim was incurred and the consideration therefor; when claim is contingent, unliquidated, disputed, subject to setoff, evidenced by a judgment, negotiable instrument, or other writing, or incurred as partner or joint contractor, so indicate; specify name of any partner or joint contractor on any debt	Amount of claim	
		$	
Leverett Furniture 125 Oak Ave. Alto, Penn. 17111	For household furniture, including two single beds and one dresser, purchased in February, 1974.	300	00
Linda's Linoleum 16 West Street Profundo, Penn. 18333	For purchase and installation of new kitchen floor materials September 10, 1974	210	00
Master Charge 21 East Street Alto, Penn. 16333	Miscellaneous small purchases, including one set golf clubs ($125.00), clothing, beverages, books, gifts, tobacco, slip covers for furniture, toys, etc.	700	00
Dan's Garage 61 Market Road Alto, Penn. 17111	Car repair October 21, 1974: engine overhaul and transmission repair	200	00
Last National Bank Main Street Alto, Penn. 17111	Personal loan for special educational expenses (books and tutors for son during his recovery from a recent operation)	750	00
Community Hospital Alto, Penn. 17111	Medical expenses for son's appendectomy	450	00
	Total	2610	00

© 1973 BY JULIUS BLUMBERG, INC., 80 EXCHANGE PL., N.Y.C. 10004

*Forms available from the publisher, Julius Blumberg, Inc., 80 Exchange Place, N.Y., N.Y. 10004.

121

Schedule A-3 — Creditors Having Unsecured Claims Without Priority

Name of creditor (including last known holder of any negotiable instrument) and residence or place of business (if unknown, so state)	Specify when claim was incurred and the consideration therefor; when claim is contingent, unliquidated, disputed, subject to setoff, evidenced by a judgment, negotiable instrument, or other writing, or incurred as partner or joint contractor, so indicate; specify name of any partner or joint contractor on any debt	Amount of claim	
	Brought forward	$ 2610	00
Discount Draperies P.O. Box 41 Alto, Penn. 17111	draperies for apartment, purchased August 10, 1974	120	00
Acme Collection Bureau P.O. Box 1001 Pittsburgh, Penn. 12345	Agent for Discount Draperies	duplicate	
Earl Doe, Sr. Output, Penn. 17666	Personal loan, February 2, 1975	200	00
Alice's Nursery School Yellow Brick Road Alto, Penn. 17111	Child care	220	00
	Total	3150	00

QF 6: Schedule A-3

© 1973 BY JULIUS BLUMBERG, INC., 80 EXCHANGE PL., N.Y.C. 10004

SCHEDULE B — STATEMENT OF ALL PROPERTY OF BANKRUPT*

Schedules B-1, B-2, B-3, and B-4 must include all property of the bankrupt as of the date of the filing of the petition by or against him.

Schedule B-1 — Real Property

Description and location of all real property in which bankrupt has an interest (including equitable and future interests, interests in estates by the entirety, community property, life estates, lease-holds, and rights and powers exercisable for his own benefit)	Nature of interest (specify all deeds and written instruments relating thereto)	Market value of bankrupt's interest without deduction for secured claims listed in schedule A-2 or exemptions claimed in schedule B-4
		$
NONE		NONE
	Total	

Schedule B-2 — Personal Property

Type of Property	Description and location	Market value of bankrupt's interest without deduction for secured claims listed on schedule A-2 or exemptions claimed in schedule B-4	
a. Cash on hand	$19.00 in household money	$ 19	00
b. Deposits of money with banking institutions, savings and loan associations, credit unions, public utility companies, landlords, and others	Last National Bank, Alto, Checking account	32	45
	Alto Savings & Loan, Savings account	11	00
c. Household goods, supplies, and furnishings	Furniture and other household goods at home approx.	700	00
d. Books, pictures, and other art objects; stamp, coin, and other collections	Approx. 35 high school social studies textbooks, one set encylopedias, several educational psychology books	aprx.100	00
e. Wearing apparel, jewelry, firearms, sports equipment, and other personal possessions	personal clothing at home. approx.	150	00
	One .22 caliber rifle.	35	00
f. Automobiles, trucks, trailers, and other vehicles	1972 Pontiac Ventura approx.	1100	00
g. Boats, motors, and their accessories	None		
	Total	2147	45

OF 6: Schedule B-1 & B-2

© 1973 by JULIUS BLUMBERG, INC., 80 EXCHANGE PL., N.Y.C. 10004

*Forms available from the publisher, Julius Blumberg, Inc., 80 Exchange Place, N.Y., N.Y. 10004.

123

Schedule B-2 — Personal Property (Continued)

Type of property	Description and location	Market value of bankrupt's interest without deduction for secured claims listed on schedule A-2 or exemptions claimed in schedule B-4	
		Brought forward	2147	45
h. Livestock, poultry, and other animals	None	$ none	
i. Farming supplies and implements	None	none	
j. Office equipment, furnishings, and supplies	none	none	
k. Machinery, fixtures, equipment, and supplies (other than those listed in items j and l) used in business	none	none	
l. Inventory	none	none	
m. Tangible personal property of any other description	Portable sewing machine	approx.90	00
n. Patents, copyrights, franchises, and other general intangibles (specify all documents and writings relating thereto)	none	none	
o. Government and corporate bonds and other negotiable and nonnegotiable instruments	none	none	
p. Other liquidated debts owing bankrupt or debtor	none	none	
q. Contingent and unliquidated claims of every nature, including counterclaims of the bankrupt or debtor (give estimated value of each)	Pension funds with Alto Department of Education; amount unknown Possible refund from 1975 income taxes	unknown unknown	
r. Interests in insurance policies (itemize surrender or refund values of each)	Health, accident and disability policy through employer	unknown	
s. Annuities	none	none	
t. Stocks and interests in incorporated and unincorporated companies (itemize separately)	none	none	
u. Interests in partnerships	none	none	
v. Equitable and future interests, life estates, and rights or powers exercisable for the benefit of the bankrupt or debtor (specify all written instruments relating thereto)	none	none	
	Total	2237	45

OF 6: Schedule B-2 (Continued)

© 1973 BY JULIUS BLUMBERG, INC., 80 EXCHANGE PL., N.Y.C. 10004

SUMMARY OF DEBTS AND PROPERTY *
(From the statements of the bankrupt in Schedule A and B)

Schedule	Debts and property	Total
	DEBTS	
A—1/a	Wages having priority	0
A—1/b(1)	Taxes owing United States	0
A—1/b(2)	Taxes owing States	0
A—1/b(3)	Taxes owing other taxing authorities ...Town of Alto	32.00
A—1/c(1)	Debts having priority by laws of the United States	0
A—1/c(2)	Rent having priority under State law	0
A—2	Secured claims	2850.00
A—3	Unsecured claims without priority	3150.00
	Schedule A total	6032.00
	PROPERTY	
B—1	Real property (total value)	0
B—2/a	Cash on hand	19.00
B—2/b	Deposits	43.45
B—2/c	Household goods	700.00
B—2/d	Books, pictures, and collections	100.00
B—2/e	Wearing apparel and personal possessions	185.00
B—2/f	Automobiles and other vehicles	1100.00
B—2/g	Boats, motors, and accessories	0
B—2/h	Livestock and other animals	0
B—2/i	Farming supplies and implements	0
B—2/j	Office equipment and supplies	0
B—2/k	Machinery, equipment, and supplies used in business	0
B—2/l	Inventory	0
B—2/m	Other tangible personal property	90.00
B—2/n	Patents and other general intangibles	0
B—2/o	Bonds and other instruments	0
B—2/p	Other liquidated debts	0
B—2/q	Contingent and unliquidated claims	unknown
B—2/r	Interests in insurance policies	unknown
B—2/s	Annuities	0
B—2/t	Interests in corporations and unincorporated companies	0
B—2/u	Interests in partnerships	0
B—2/v	Equitable and future interests, rights, and powers in personality	0
B—3/a	Property assigned for benefit of creditors	0
B—3/b	Property not otherwise scheduled	
B—4	Property claimed as exempt $ 402.65	XXXXXXXXXX
	Schedule B total	2237.45

OATHS TO SCHEDULES A AND B

State of   Pennsylvannia   County of   Lincoln   ss.:   April 1, 1965

Individual: I   John Robert Doe   do hereby swear that I have read the foregoing schedules, consisting of 6 sheets, and that they are a statement of all my debts and all my property in accordance with the Bankruptcy Act, to the best of my knowledge, information, and belief.

~~Corporation~~

~~xxxxxxxxx x xxxx xxx xxxxxxxxx xxxxxxxxxxx~~
~~xxpropexty xxk thx xxxpxxxxtixxx xx xxxxxxxxx x xtx thx Bxxkxxpxxy xtxx xx xxx~~

~~Partnership~~

~~xthxxxxxxxxxxxxxx xxxxgxxxx xxkxdxxxx xxxxxxxxx xx~~
~~xxxxxx thx xxxxxxxxx xx xxxx xxxxxx xxth thx Bxxkxxpxxx xxt x tx thx bxxt xfxxxxxkxxxxxdxx~~

~~hxx xxxxxxxxxxxxxx xx xxxx x fxxx xx xx xxxxxxxxxx xxxxx agxxt~~
~~of thx xxxpxxxxtixxxx bxxk xxpxx ixx thix pxxxxxdxxgx xx hxxxby~~
~~xxxx, xxd thxt thxy xxx x xtxtxmxxtxf xxx thx dxbtx xxxx xxk thx~~
~~xxxxxxxx xxk thxxx xxxxxxxxx txx thx bxxt xfxxxy kxxxxxxgx ixfxxxxtixx xxx bxxixf~~

~~x jxxxxxxxx xxx xxxxxxxxxxxxxxxt xgxxxy~~
~~of thx partnership nxxxd xx bxxkxxpx xx thix prxxxxdxxg dx hxxxby xwxxx~~
~~thxxx xxd thxt thxy xxx x xtxtxmxxt xfxxx thx xxbtx xxd xxx thx prxp~~

Subscribed and sworn to before me on
April 1, 1975

(Notary Seal)

Signed   *John Robert Doe*

Mary R. Roe

Mary R. Roe, Notary Public
My commission expires 5-11-78.

official character

* In the opinion of the bankrupt-debtor the net value of the non-exempt assets will not exceed $150.00.

OF 6: Summary of debts & property: oaths
© 1973 BY JULIUS BLUMBERG, INC., 80 EXCHANGE PL., N.Y.C. 10004

(To be signed if applicable)

* Massachusetts District requires this statement, if applicable. Other Districts may require this or similar statements.

*Forms available from the publisher, Julius Blumberg, Inc., 80 Exchange Place, N.Y., N.Y. 10004.

HOW TO GET OUT OF DEBT

United States District Court for the Western   District of   Pennsylvannia *

In re JOHN ROBERT DOE, a/k/a John R. Doe, J. Robert Doe, J.R. Doe, Jack Doe	*BANKRUPTCY NO.*
	STATEMENT
SSN 123-45-6789 Bankrupt Include here all names used by bankrupt within last 6 years.	Pursuant to Rule 219(b)

The undersigned, pursuant to Rule 219 (b), Rules of Bankruptcy Procedure, states that the compensation paid or promised by the bankrupt(s), to the undersigned, is as follows:

For legal services rendered (including spouse if both file), Bankrupt agreed to pay .... $...NONE..........

Prior to the filing of this Statement, Bankrupt (and spouse if applicable) has paid the undersigned .... $.........................

Balance due .... $.........................

The filing fee has—*has not* been paid.

The services rendered or to be rendered include the following:

(a) Analysis of the financial situation, and rendering advice and assistance to the client in determining whether to file a petition under the Bankruptcy Act.

(b) Preparation and filing of the petition, schedules of assets and liabilities, and statement of affairs.

(c) Representation of the client at the first meeting of creditors.

The undersigned further states that the source of monies paid by the Bankrupt(s) to the undersigned was and is, earnings, wages and compensation for services performed, and

The undersigned further states that the undersigned has not shared, or agreed to share with any other person, other than with members of undersigned's law firm, any compensation, except as herein after set forth.

Dated:

Respectfully submitted,

....................................Not..applicable...................................
Attorney for Petitioner

Address   ....

....

T 1048—Statement of compensation: Rule 219(b)   © 1973 by JULIUS BLUMBERG, INC., 80 EXCHANGE PL., N.Y.C. 10004

*Forms available from the publisher, Julius Blumberg, Inc., 80 Exchange Place, N.Y., N.Y. 10004.

APPENDIX F | SPECIMEN PETITION FOR STRAIGHT BANKRUPTCY PROCEEDINGS

UNITED STATES DISTRICT COURT FOR THE Western   DISTRICT OF   Pennsylvannia*

In re   JOHN ROBERT DOE, a/k/a John R. Doe, J. Robert   ) BANKRUPTCY NO.
       Doe, J.R. Doe, Jack Doe

       SSN 123-45-6789   Bankrupt)
Include here all names used by bankrupt within last 6 years.

LIST OF CREDITORS

Acme Collection Bureau P.O. Box 1001 Pittsburgh, Penn. 12345	Linda's Linoleum 16 West Street Alto, Penn. 17111
Alice's Nursery School Yellow Brick Road Alto, Penn. 17111	Master Charge 21 East Street Alto, Penn. 16333
Alto, Town of Town Hall Alto, Penn. 17111	White's Dept. Store 200 Main Street Tenor, Penn. 19222
Community Hospital Alto, Penn. 17111	
Dan's Garage 61 Market Road Alto, Penn. 17111	
Discount Draperies P.O. Box 41 Alto, Penn. 17111	
Earl Doe, Sr. Output, Penn. 17666	
Friendly Finance 18 South Street Alto, Penn. 17111	
Last National Bank Main Street Alto, Penn. 17111	
Leverett Furniture 125 Oak Ave. Alto, Penn. 17111	

S 1051—Creditors List

© 1973 BY JULIUS BLUMBERG, INC., 80 EXCHANGE PL., N.Y.C. 10004

*Forms available from the publisher, Julius Blumberg, Inc., 80 Exchange Place, N.Y., N.Y. 10004.

127

About the Author

Daniel Kaufman, a graduate of Amherst College and a freelance writer and photographer, found himself facing a mound of personal debts. Being without funds, he went to a library instead of a lawyer. Since he couldn't find a straightforward guide to his rights as a debtor, he decided to research and write this book, working closely with a lawyer friend. He solved his financial problems in the process and hopes to do the same for you.

Readers' Notes

The following blank pages have been provided for the readers' personal computations.